The Impossible Only Takes a Little Longer

One Woman's Story of Determination

Sheila Radziewicz

To Eddy

Remember anything is possible

Sheila Radziewicz Hayworth

The Impossible Only Takes a Little Longer

One Woman's Story of Determination

Sheila Radziewicz

Boston, Massachusetts
2014

The Impossible Only Takes a Little Longer may be
purchased in bulk. For more information, email
Sheila Radziewicz at sheila@findthefierce.com

Cover Photography by Shane Ernest
www.rarerthan.com

Publisher: CreateSpace Self Publishing
Boston, Massachusetts

Library of Congress Cataloging-in-Publication Data

Sheila Radziewicz, 1978 -
   [The Impossible Only Takes a Little Longer]
   The Impossible Only Takes a Little Longer / Sheila Radziewicz
   ISBN10: 1494494701
   ISBN13: 978-1494494704

Printed in the USA

About Sheila Radziewicz

Award winning advocate, speaker and educator, Sheila Radziewicz has faced inequality, fought against institutional discrimination and questions society's norms. She has educated others about disabilities by simply being herself and by answering questions. She has stood up against institutional discrimination when going to college and getting her drivers license because she understood the importance of being the voice of the people. She has been encouraged to experience life to the fullest and do anything and everything possible by her incredibly supportive family.

Sheila is dedicated and determined advocate with a Masters Degree in Criminal Justice. Her bright personality, ability and determination are so apparent that you may not even realize she has a disability. Today Sheila is an advocate for people with disabilities, drives a car with her feet and has been featured in newspapers and radio stations national and international for earning her Black Belt in Tae Kwon Do.

Currently Sheila works at the Northeast Independent Living Program providing advocacy within systems to empower persons with disabilities to achieve vocational goals. Sheila was a Volunteer Coordinator at Healing Abuse Working for Change (HAWC) an agency which supports individuals experiencing domestic violence. There she supported clients with restraining orders, informed them about their rights, and offered other resources. She also trained criminal justice agencies, civil organizations and other community members on effects of domestic violence, legal advocacy, disability awareness and many other topics.

As a motivational speaker, Sheila's confidence and ability is spellbinding. She has made some laugh and others cry. Her written story is something you will remember for years to come. This dynamic individual will inspire and motivate you to make changes in your life.

Table of Contents

Acknowledgment i

Introduction v

Chapter One: Braces, Oh Braces 1

Chapter Two: Inspiration 13

Chapter Three: Perceptions of Life 25

Chapter Four: The Mirror 39

Chapter Five: Advocating through Ignorance 59

Chapter Six: True Independence 77

Chapter Seven: The Giver 90

Chapter Eight: Driving Forward 111

Chapter Nine: Front Page News 121

Chapter Ten: Accepting Myself 131

Chapter Eleven: The Way 139

Chapter Twelve: Disability Not! 165

Acknowledgments

As I look back on my life there is one common theme and that is support. I truly believe that I would never have accomplished all of the things that I've done in my life had it not been for my amazing network of support. It is not possible for me to list everyone but there are a few that I feel are important to highlight.

I owe my first thanks to my mom, Mary Radziewicz, and my dad, John Radziewicz. They have loved me unconditionally and continue to support me through everything I've ever tried my life. I've always believed that I was born with a feisty personality and my parents helped foster that which has helped me with my success in life. They have always been there and continue to be there for the hardest times in my life and the best. There are not enough words to truly express the gratitude that I have for my parents. I know that they endured many hardships in order to make sure that I succeeded in life and for that I am deeply grateful.

My sisters Lisa Tucker and Christine LeBlanc are two people that have always been there for me. Both of them have been there to stand up for me and laugh with me. You know you have great sisters when they agreed to play tea party with you ever though that is the last thing in the world they are interested in doing. As sisters we've stuck together through thick and thin. It is always been awesome to know that when I needed someone they were there and continue to be.

Shriners Hospital for Children is an organization that is amazing! The comprehensive medical care and support that me and my family received has impacted all of our lives significantly. The free medical care for all of my surgeries, braces and outpatient services allowed my family to focus on us and not financial hardships. Shriners Hospital also gave us a community of people and hope. There is one doctor that I will always hold close to my heart and that is Dr Leon Kruger (1923-2007). He gave my family hope when no one else would. He made a promise to my family and succeeded beyond all of our imagination. It was his direction and guidance that has made walking possible for me. I am deeply grateful for everything that he gave me and my family.

There are also four friends that have helped me in making my dream of writing my book possible. Julie Atlas, a woman I meet in graduate school, who has come one of my closest friend. My partner in crime while we wrote our thesis was quick to answer my call for help with editing. Deborah Edinburg a friend and volunteer at my work HAWC heard about my writing and offered her experience as I took my writing to next level and motivated me to continue going forward with my dream. Just when I had hit another road block another friend stepped forward Nicole Richon- Schoel. She said "I'm here to help you with your final edits". Her experience and her talents have bought my to an even higher level and for that I'm grateful. Last, Eva Montibello has been the nuts and bolts in this self publishing process. She has pushed me to make decisions and has taught me some much over the over the last year. Without her this book would still be in a Word document!

There are also the hundreds of people who have impacted my life for years and brought me so much love. I'm thankful to have so many communities that have supported me through the years. They have been there for me in the hard times and the good. My extended family grandparents, aunts, uncles, and cousins. Have helped so much and given so much love. My childhood neighborhood of Salem Street in Malden I have so many amazing memories. Everyone from the Boston Minuteman Campground in Littleton Massachusetts thank you and I love you. Then there is my tribe many who I've met through Drum and Dance Cambridge, Spiritfire, Wildfire and through Earth Spirit Events. The support all of you have given me has made so much of a difference I would not be the woman I am today had it not been for all of you.

Finally I'd like to thank Bruce McCorry and Sandra LaRosa. These two people came into my life less than a decade ago and have seen me through some amazing changes. Their belief in me and support was the catalyst to the writing of a story in the local newspaper which changed my life. Media and letters swarmed their business and they took it in stride. Continuously finding ways to support me so that I could share my story to the world. They both even found time to give me some worldly advice when all the attention got a little overwhelming. Their support and friendship is something I am grateful to have in my life.

To all of you and everything that you have given and never asked for in return. I am a strong, determined, independent woman because of all of you! Now you all can stop asking me when are you going to write that book Sheila. Here it is! I hope all you enjoy it as much as I enjoyed writing it. Light love and positive energy to all of you. Blessed be!

A disability is not a disease… it is a state of being. If you have a disability it means that you get to live in a world that does not know and will not NEVER ever truly understand what it is like to be you. I grew up thinking that I had two choices in life: one, to live each day to the fullest and succeed no matter what; and two, to feel sorry for myself and do nothing. I have chosen to live each day to its fullest, and I have succeeded in just about everything I have ever wanted to do. It has not been easy and there has been pain and suffering. I have done things in my life because I wanted to do them. Other times, I pushed myself because I needed to prove another person or system wrong. My family and friends will tell you that the best way to help me succeed is to tell me I will not be able to do something.

Believing in myself is how I have made it in life. I think it is important for people to believe in themselves, and if you really want something you need to be prepared for the fact that it might take some time. We are all going to have hard times and sometimes we need to just cry… and then get up and start again. Each of us has the power to live our lives, as we want to live them; we just need to accept the challenges around us and move forward. For as long as I can remember, my mother had a motto for me: "Nothing is impossible, for the impossible only takes a little longer". This has become my mantra. It has kept me from giving up when times have been hard, and it has enabled me to see the positive and find the light at the end of the tunnel. I am alive despite what the doctors said, and my story continues. I have accomplished so many things that people said I could not or should not do. I have achieved so much, and I have done it with the love and support of friends, family, and a network of amazing people. Here is my story.

When I was born the medical professionals predicted that I would not live longer than a week. My family had me baptized by a nurse and I was given last rites within days of my birth. All the predictions were wrong, and I went on living against all odds. I was born with a rare genetic congenital birth defect known as Thrombocytopenia absent radius, or TAR syndrome. TAR syndrome is characterized by low levels of platelets in the blood and the absence of both the long, thin bones of the forearms and the presence of the thumb. Other abnormalities can include additional skeletal anomalies, such as the absence or underdevelopment of the other bones of the forearm, the infusion of the knee joints and the absence of the kneecaps, along with heart and kidney anomalies.

I was born April 30, 1978, the third daughter in a family of five. The first year of my life was a struggle. My medical problems came as a shock to everyone. Neither my doctors nor my parents had any idea that I would be born with a disability. I had a hole in my heart, low platelets and I was missing eight bones: my humerus, radius, ulna, and patella, on both sides of my body. My feet were rotated inward, my hips were dislocated, and I had intolerance to cow's milk. Doctors expected the worst, telling my parents it was unlikely that I would survive. As the days and weeks went by, to everyone's surprise, I continued to thrive.

My parent's experience with the doctors was both amazing and horrific. My mom's OBGYN was supportive and understanding. He told my dad to go home, get some rest and inform the rest of the family. My mother was sedated due to the emergency C-section that was performed to deliver me, so the doctor suggested that my dad use this time to regroup. Unfortunately, the hospital pediatrician was emotionally inept, treating me like something other than human when he brought me to my father. When my mother was alone, the pediatrician brought me to her despite my father's instruction to stay away from her. There was no one close to her to help her cope with the shock that I was born with this life-threatening disability. She remembers that moment of extreme apprehension and fear, but was joined by my father and our family, and they held each other together

I was finally able to come home from the hospital, but my stay was short-lived. I returned to the hospital, where I remained until just before Thanksgiving. This extended stay was related to my milk intolerance and the hole in my heart. My extended family gave as much support as they could. My grandparents would watch my sisters when we had medical appointments. Sometimes my grandmother would go with my mom and me when my dad had to work. My parents have told me that after I was born my pediatrician, Dr. Lou Bartoshesky, family doctor had a particularly critical conversation with them. He said, "You have two choices with your daughter. Either you do everything for her now and in the future, or you give her the tools to become independent." My parents selected the latter. This was the turning point for them. They knew what they needed to do, despite how hard it was going to be for everyone.

Chapter 1
Braces, Oh Braces

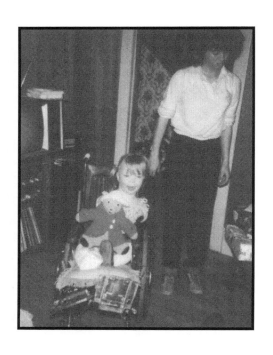

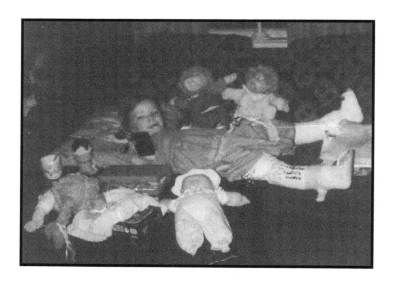

I Am Not

Mangled, frail, delicate infant
Weak, poor, ignorant infant, I was not!

You did not have the power
to define my fate with Death

Cripple, feeble minded, pitiful child
Unable, immobile, lame child, I was not!

I defied your prediction, then
I deny your position, now

Undetermined, incapable, paralyzed woman
Lessen, negative, powerless woman, I am not!

Fear forced your prediction of my Death
Fear created your insecurity
Fear does not rule me

Complete, strong, unbreakable infant
Bold, healthy, aware infant, I was!

I chose to prove you wrong
The power to live was mine

Whole, intelligent, witty, child
Able, mobile, bright child, I was!

I believed in myself
I knew success was coming

Determined, capable, secure woman
Brave, confident, powerful woman, I am!

I fought against your fear
I fought against your insecurity
I chose life when you would not!

*M*y medical history is colorful and lengthy. Born in Malden, Massachusetts I was immediately transferred to Floating Hospital in Boston. It was vital that I receive immediate medical care in order to survive. There were three immediate medical concerns: the hole in my heart, my low platelet count, and my intolerance to cow's milk.

The hole in my heart was a grave concern and difficult to correct, due to my low platelets, which made surgery dangerous. There was a possibility that I could bleed out. Rather than risk the surgery, the doctors took a less invasive approach and chose to monitor my heart. As time went on, my body began to heal, and slowly the hole closed itself. In May 1983, I was discharged from the cardiology clinic with what doctors referred to as a "functional heart murmur". The murmur was not an issue for me until I was sixteen and trying out for my school soccer team. I was confused, because although my knees were feeling great I was having difficult time breathing. When I told my mother, she casually mentioned that the breathing problem probably had something to do with my heart murmur. I suppose the murmur was the least of her concerns when I was younger so she had forgotten about it.

A key characteristic of TAR Syndrome is the presence of Thrombocytopenia, a low level of platelets. The condition of Thrombocytopenia made it necessary for me to have a blood transfusion within the first few days of my life. I was monitored regularly for bleeding in my skin and for brain hemorrhages. The monitoring was imperative because the major cause of death with TAR Syndrome is bleeding episodes. As I grew, the platelet concern decreased, although I continued to have frequent nosebleeds and bruised easily. In October of 1981, my platelet count became stable at 81,000. I am unsure of the average platelet count of a child but a normal adult count ranges from 150,000 to 450,000. My normal range is currently 80,000 to 125,000. This is quite a bit lower than the norm, but my body has been able to adapt.

The final concern for doctors at this time was my intolerance to milk, along with my esophageal reflux. I was hospitalized twice within the first two years of my life to treat this problem. The first hospitalization lasted approximately seven months and was specifically for the milk intolerance. I was given a lamb oil glucose formula, but was found to have no tolerance for that, either, and subsequently needed to be hospitalized for about seven months. At some point between the ages of three and five years my intolerance ended and I have not had a problem since.

When I was about two years old my medical care began to change. Now that my life- threatening issues were under control, it was time to tackle my orthopedic needs. My parents decided to investigate a hospital that gave free medical care to children with disabilities, called Shriners Hospital for Children. One Shriners Hospital is located in Massachusetts and was two and a half hours from my house. An appointment was made, and when we arrived, my parents were finally given the hope we all needed. During a meeting with the Chief of Staff, Dr. Kruger, he told them that I would walk one day.

When I entered kindergarten, I ambled into school without a walker or metal braces. Shriners Hospital became a second home to me, a place where I spent countless hours and always felt safe. The doctors and nurses were amazing, and the other children and their families understood what I was going through, which helped me deal with the pain. Dr. Kruger went right to work on his promise that I would walk. My orthopedic care involved leg braces, a walker and several major surgeries.

I have many memories of Shriners Hospital. I had most of my care at the old hospital, which was a brick building that contained a large, open clinic room and stretched back to a school. As a child I was very curious, and always asked questions. I remember how Dr. Kruger would stop everything and answer my questions. He always made it known to the students at clinic that a patient's questions were the first priority, even if she was only five years old. I remember bringing pictures to him at every visit, and I always felt that I was his favorite patient. As an adult looking back, I know many of us felt the same, and this was an important gift. I felt listened to. I was never afraid of going to the doctor, and believe me, I had reason to be afraid. Every visit put me one step closer to a surgery or included surgery itself. It brought me one step closer to being able to walk, and later, to walk without leg braces. The visits and surgeries also brought me closer to being able to do the same things that my friends could do, and that was very important to me.

In winter of 1981, a promise became true. For months I had been wearing night braces to strengthen and straighten my legs, and I spent three weeks in traction to correct my hip dislocation. My mobility was hampered, but I continued to move around either by riding my mini-bike or scooting on the floor. I had even begun to walk on my knees. Then in November, I received leg braces, a walker, and a soft cloth helmet. With these tools, I was able to walk. The process was slow and my teachers or parents stayed close because they were concerned that I might fall and not be able to catch myself. The procedure was tiring and frustrating. The other children could go so much faster, and I really did not like the helmet. This was the beginning of a long road. Soon I would have surgery on both legs multiple times and then, with time, I would walk without the aid of a walker or braces.

During the spring of 1982, Shriners performed the first of many surgeries on my legs. They did two that year… one on each leg, with the purpose of transferring a hamstring. It was difficult to be independently mobile that year, but we soon got creative. My parents gave me a Cookie Monster scooter, and I would use whichever leg had not had surgery to push the scooter. This was better than a wheelchair, which required the assistance of others. I became extremely proficient on my scooter, especially when both

4

legs were without casts. The surgeries and inpatient care would continue until I was about nine.

I spent one Christmas in a body cast, following my nastiest surgery in the winter of 1985. I had been scheduled for surgery on both legs, so I expected that I would have casts on both of my legs from the tops of my thighs to my toes, but I did not know all of the facts. When I woke up in Recovery, the room was dark and I had an IV in my hand. I felt very stiff and quickly realized that I could not move my waist and hips. I looked down and saw a cast starting at the top of my chest and going all the way down my legs, with only my toes free. My legs were spread apart with a piece of wood connecting them. There were metal pins coming out of the cast at two points on both outer thighs. I cried when I realized that I was confined in a body cast.

At a later time it was explained to me that it had been necessary to place the cast a certain number of inches above and below the surgical point, and therefore the body cast was required. I did not care why this body cast had to be on me, I only knew that it made my life even more difficult. It felt so unfair!

Playing with toys was one of many issues I faced. Now I had only my hands to use. At one point a Lego fell into the cast and the nurses had to get a hanger to fish it out. Breathing was difficult, so the doctors decided to cut a hole in the cast around my bellybutton and this allowed me to breathe easily. Sleeping was horrible, as moving my body was impossible. The nurses made me as comfortable as possible. They turned me to sleep alternately on my stomach and my back at least once a night. The operation was just before Christmas, and I assumed that I would be spending Christmas in the hospital.

I remember the Christmas party in the girls' ward. There was music, food, presents and Santa. I was having a lot of fun when my dad and uncle showed up. They had come to take me home for Christmas. The next thing I knew I was in the back of my uncle's station wagon, going home. I was so excited to be going home for Christmas. It was hard for me to be so limited in movement. My family put my toys on my cast and played with me. At night my Light-Bright doll was put halfway into the dresser drawer so I could see it lit.

The most frightening experience with the body cast was getting it removed. The sound and vibrations of removing the cast was terrifying and the pain medications they gave me never seemed to work. When the cast was removed I saw metal pins sticking out from my thighs, but until that moment I did not know that the pins were in my legs. The next thing I remember is screaming as loud as I could. Later, my mom said they could hear me down the hall. I still don't remember how the pins were removed, but I assume they came out at that time because I do not remember going back into surgery. My dad remembers them removing the cast while I was awake and then putting me to sleep to remove the pins.

My last surgery was performed when I was in the third grade, and it was desperately needed. This surgery was to correct the buckling of my right knee. The buckling was frightening because without notice my knee would collapse, and I would end up on the floor in the worst possible pain. If I was not standing when my knee gave out I would not have to worry about falling, but the knee pain would follow anyway. I feared that I might fall down the stairs or break a bone. The pain would bring me to tears in a second, which was unusual, as I had a high pain tolerance due to all the procedures I had endured. As a child, when I had surgery I was put in a wheelchair or on my Cookie Monster scooter, and I was fine with that… until my cousin Stephen hurt his ankle.

I remember Stephen using crutches and wondering if I could use them, too, so I asked him and he gave them to me without a second thought. Stephen and I spent lots of time together and he knew I could do everything that he could do. At first I was not sure how the crutches would work, since I could not reach the handgrips. Then I realized I could hold the top beneath the under-arm grip. This worked pretty well as long as I was not using them for a long time. I got the hang of it quickly, and then we started really playing. We set the crutches to their tallest setting and then used them to fly across the room. It is a miracle that I did not hurt something in the process. A few months later I went in for surgery.

After mastering crutches, I felt certain I did not need a wheelchair, and I mentioned this to the nurses. They did not agree. I decided to wait for "rounds" the next day, to talk to Dr. Kruger. I figured he would say I could use crutches and the nurses would have to agree to it. The next day I explained to Dr. Kruger that I could use crutches and therefore did not need a wheelchair. I showed him how I could operate them and he said to go ahead and use them. I was very excited, but unfortunately, the nurses still only let me use them when someone was by my side. As you may have guessed, I came up with an alternative. While waiting for what seemed like forever to be wheeled to the other side of the girls' ward, I looked at my crutches and realized how I could do it. I used the crutches as you would use oars in a boat, and pushed myself to the other ward. It was a slow process and was not the easiest thing I have ever done, but it got me where I wanted to go. It was fun to confound the nurses. When they finally came looking for me, I was gone!

As a child I spent far too many months in casts. Most of the time I dealt with it well, but not always. After one surgery I did not want to be in the cast, and I was determined to get out of it. After being sent home from the hospital in my cast, I decided that I had enough of it, so I wiggled my leg out. You would think that would tricky, but one must understand that the cast was like a brace to me. I spent years in braces, and when I wanted to get out of them without anyone around I would slide my foot out without any problem. When they realized what I had done, the "powers that be" were less than pleased, for a couple of reasons. First of all, I really needed to be in a cast because of the surgery on my leg, and secondly, we needed to go back to Shriners, which was a two and a half hour drive from home. We took the trip back to Shriners and they put me in a cast for the second time. Even though I understood how important it was for me to be in this cast, I still did not like it. At the next opportunity, I wiggled myself out of the cast again. Back to Shriners we went, so they could put me back in a cast for the third time. This time they got smart and glued me in the cast. They sent me home with the hope that I might keep it on longer this time. I realized pretty quickly that I could not wiggle my leg out this time, but there were other ways of getting this cast off my leg. Our house had hardwood floors, and so I lifted up my leg and bashed the cast on the ground over and over and over again. Before I knew it the cast had cracked, and I was able to get out of it yet again. This would be the final time my parents drove me to Shriners and I got my fourth cast. My parents were not happy with me, nor were the hospital staff. They made it very clear that this cast was to stay on my leg and I was to stop the nonsense. I listened that time, despite how unhappy it made me.

All the surgeries I underwent were geared to impact my walking ability positively, and each one was followed with the fitting of new leg braces. The fittings were frightening at first, so some of the staff tried to make a game of it. They put smiley faces on my knees and made a train track up my legs where the saw was used to remove the cast fitting, and they made train sounds as the saw went all the way up. The braces were necessary to give my legs support and strength. Through the years I had many different kinds of leg braces, because I was a very active child and often broke them. I remember the braces being very uncomfortable, especially in the summer. I had to be dressed in stockings or tights when wearing the braces; or else my skin would stick to the plastic in the braces. The summer heat, combined with my braces and tights, would produce rashes and itching galore. My parents were told that I was to wear them unless I was sleeping or in physical therapy. Luckily, my parents believed physical therapy should involve more than just time with the physical therapist, so it included riding my mini wheel and later, Big Wheel, and also swimming and other activities.

As important as it was for me to wear my braces, it was also important for me not to wear braces. Having your hands at your shoulders can make some things more difficult than others. I understood when I was very young that I needed to use more than my hands to do things; therefore, my feet have always been a second set of hands for me. If I was on the floor I would use my toes, and if I was standing or at a table, I would use my fingers. I learned to slide my braces on and off without even removing the Velcro, so I could do things with my feet and then get the braces back on. I never liked my braces. They were made of metal, plastic, and Velcro. Although they made some things easier, and a lot of things became more difficult with them.

Walking was easier when I had the braces on, and I could walk longer distances and go faster. They often made the pain go away as well, but I never liked them and did not want to wear them. Braces also prevented me from wearing the clothing that I wanted to wear. You might think that being able to walk was more important than what I could or could not wear. But back then fitting in was the most important thing for me. I knew I was different and did not want to be any more different than I had to be. I always wore my braces under my pants so I could hide them, and I tried to get away with not wearing them if at all possible. I was very excited when they would break. Unfortunately, my dad had spare parts at the house to fix them so we did not have to drive to Shriners. I wore ugly sneakers with the braces because of the plastic piece around my foot, and because I could not reach to tie my shoes, I had to have Velcro. One of the worst things about the braces was that they squeaked. I had to put oil on my braces like the Tin Man in "The Wizard of Oz". It was embarrassing. If the squeak started at home it was not a big deal, but if I was at school I had to wait until I got home to fix the squeaking.

After one of my surgeries, the doctors informed me that not only did I have to wear the braces again, but at this point I would have to walk around with straight legs. This straight leg walking was a bit of a concern for me. My bedroom was on the second floor. My school classroom was also on the second floor. Neither my house nor my school had an elevator. Part of my physical therapy for the next few weeks was learning to walk up and down stairs straight-legged. I was seven and I usually caught onto things pretty quickly. At first I held onto the banister. One leg went first and then I would swing the other one up. I repeated this very slowly and made it up the stairs. Within a few weeks I had the process down, and I could run up the stairs with straight knees. Walking up and down stairs straight legged was one of the many skills I learned through physical therapy. In reality, my therapy had started long ago, when my parents chose to give me the tools I needed to move toward gaining my independence.

Chapter 2
Inspiration

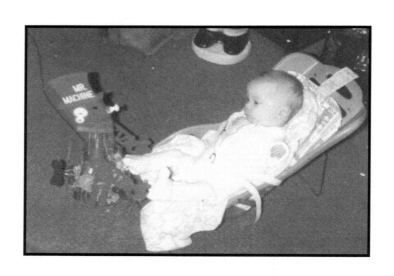

Inspiration

I am an inspiration.
Well, that is what I have been told

Right from the start I defied the world
Why? You ask… because I wanted to survive
And not just survive, but truly live

I am an inspiration.
I took the world on and I did it with love, smiles and giggles
I took on every challenge like it was puzzle
and I wanted to see the final picture

You are an inspiration.
You took on the world with your words and actions as I watched

You were there at the start of everything
Cheering me on and providing strength, confidence and love

You are an inspiration.
You gave me everything unconditionally and never looked back

You are the inspirational ones.
I am merely living by your example

*W*hen I was an infant, my parents made the difficult and courageous choice to do everything they could to provide me with the tools to become independent. Their insistence and perseverance was the critical first step on my life journey. As a young child I received services which were available in large part due to two pieces of legislation: the Rehabilitation Act of 1973, Section 504 which requires schools to provide "free appropriate public education", and the Americans with Disabilities Act.

Beginning at age two, I received services appropriate for my needs in school. I started with the Tri-City Early Intervention program, which was at a church not far from my home. There I was integrated with children of many different abilities. At the program, they worked on activities such as physical therapy, occupational therapy, social skills, dressing and feeding oneself, and playing. Help with physical skills was especially important to me, because it is common with TAR Syndrome to have delayed gross motor skills.

My early intervention program progress notes show some of my developmental milestones, and demonstrate the importance of these services. At 6 months old, I had the motor function of a 3 month old and the mental function of a 4 month old. This meant that I was just learning to grasp and shake small objects and follow moving objects or people with my eyes. At 9 months it is documented that I could hold large toys with my two feet and could sit on my own. By fourteen months I was able to "inch" forward on my bottom and transfer objects from foot to hand. At the age of about three my baby book reads that I took my first steps, holding Daddy's hand. By the age of four I was able to feed myself, color, and walk with the aid of a walker and leg braces. I was making progress toward becoming independent and slowly figuring out how I was going to do things with my little hands. This program played a large role in assisting my parents with finding an integrated preschool program.

In September 1981, I entered the Anne Sullivan School, which was a preschool program containing both children with special needs and able-bodied students. It was here that socially acceptable norms started to be put in place for me. One progress report reads, "She is being encouraged to use her hands as the socially preferred alternative to manipulating things with her feet". Some of the other progress reports comment on my ability to compensate for my disability. As well meaning as these comments might have been, they were a written reinforcement that my disability was something to be cured. As a young child I had a well-established self-image. People recognized that in me; yet it surprised people. The misconception that I had a hard life and therefore must not be a happy individual was a part of my daily reality. This stereotype would follow me throughout my childhood until the end high school, when I realized that the accepted standards of "normal" were ridiculous, and there was no reason for me to pretend to be someone I was not.

At the Anne Sullivan School in Tewksbury, Massachusetts, I had physical and occupational therapy, and I became involved in school life. I was at Anne Sullivan due to my need for the therapy, but this was not just a school. The state covered my all my expenses and transportation. The Anne Sullivan School taught me about myself in relation to other people. It served a variety of students, which helped me figure out what I needed to do in order to function independently. I do not remember being treated differently at Anne Sullivan. I was quite young so my memories of the school are few. But I do remember a young girl on my bus. Her name was Neely, and we became good friends. We both had a disability. I do not remember what her disability was, I just know that she used crutches to walk and had braces from her hips to her feet. We had a ritual of running down the hallways fast as we could, to see who would get to the bus first. Usually it ended up with a lot of giggles and laughing. I don't think we even kept count of who made it to the end of the hallway first

I also remember story time at the Anne Sullivan School. A boy named David liked to sit next to me at story time. For some reason, whenever he sat down, I would get up with my mat and move. He would follow me. The teacher made us stop and usually we ended up sitting next to each other anyway. I do remember that David was my friend. Maybe someday he will read this, and remind me why I kept moving my seat.

Then there was an exercise at snack time that never made sense to me. Perhaps a physical or occupational therapist would understand. The teachers would tape my fingers together… at least the last three, but maybe even the fourth one. I do not recall all the details but they had me eat my snack with taped fingers. I am guessing that this was part of some kind of therapy, perhaps as a way to help me with my fine motor skills. This memory still puzzles me.

The school was always finding ways to engage me in physical therapy. There was a lot of walking practice. They always made me wear a helmet and use my walker. I never enjoyed the helmet, but I was learning to walk. When I got home I would practice more, and eventually I was able to walk on my own without the walker or the helmet.

I honestly do not like the need for adaptations in my life. When I say "adaptations" I mean the need to use tools or other devices to perform daily activities. As a child I remember adults trying to give me lots of different devices to help me achieve independence. They always seemed aggravating. Why couldn't I just use my hands? Yes, I needed to do things a little differently from everybody else, but I was able to accomplish what I needed and wanted to do. I remember thinking that if I learned to do things only with many aids, then I was going have to carry paraphernalia with me every single day. The adaptations that were presented to me included bowls and silverware, a shoehorn and sock helper, as well as a raised and slanted desk at school. That desk was created twice… once when I was a child in elementary school, and again when I went to college. The second desk was far more complicated and far more useless. The pencil holders were designed so they could get me to hold my pencil "correctly", even though my fingers could not cooperate. There were various tools to assist me with washing and using the restroom that were, again, useless.

What my family and I learned from these "adaptations" was that it was okay for me to do things differently and sometimes more slowly than others did. At this point in my life I have very few special tools. I can actually only think of three: my hook, my car, and a little kitchen device my dad made for me. My hook assists me with dressing, my car so that I can drive with my feet and my kitchen device, which assists me in lifting the lid off my pots and pans. For everything else, I have simply learned to make it work.

I tell people that my world is a puzzle and I merely need to learn how to put the pieces together. That is the simple truth. I spent the first three years of my life on the ground looking up. I have had a different view of the world. I watched people and studied how they performed the daily activities of life . My Papa B. nicknamed me "Bright Eyes" because my eyes were always busy. I wanted to see everything. Once I learned to talk, my curiosity about the world expanded, with loads of questions and a determination to see and do everything possible. I began using my feet as hands from the very beginning. If I wanted something and my feet could reach it, I used them. Looking through family photos, there are numerous pictures of me aged one or two, using my feet to play with toys and dolls.

As the years went by, I received services at school as needed. Sometimes I felt comfortable with them and sometimes I did not. I tried to fit in as much as possible and I accepted assistance only when absolutely necessary. I wanted to do things on my own. This sometimes got me in trouble with my own body, as I would push myself and end up in pain. I used a hook for dressing and going to the restroom, and I remember feeling embarrassed that I took a stick to the bathroom, so I often avoided the girls' room at school. When the time came for sleepovers, I begged my parents to make me something better for traveling. I felt self-conscious and wanted a tool that was easier to hide. I would not explain that to them until I was much older.

In 1990, I enrolled in a private school and the services surrounding my disability ended. Looking back, I am not sure why the therapy stopped or why an Individual Educational Plan, (I.E.P.) was never drafted. Fortunately, the school recognized my need for "reasonable accommodations". I was given a second set of books because carrying books around was very painful. I was given extra time on tests and written assignments. The only difficulty I remember was with one of the gym teachers. When I wanted to stop or sit down, he would tell me to walk it off and keep going. We ended up having to get a doctor's note from Shriners' Hospital for Children explaining my need to stop and sit when I had knee pain. This seemed absurd to me. I would not say I was in pain when I was not.

In high school my need for reasonable accommodations was recognized. I was given a second set of books and extra time on tests and written assignments. I was excused from gym and typing class. Despite this, high school was the first time I acutely felt the sting of discrimination. . Perhaps my parents had shielded me from this, and the staring and name-calling were familiar, yet now there was a difference. I began to apply for jobs, as my friends were doing, but they were getting hired and I was not. This experience taught me that I was constantly going to have to prove myself to the world. I looked toward the future, and thought that perhaps having arms would be helpful. So I made a call to Shriners' Hospital for Children.

Shriners' afforded me all the medical care I needed for my legs, and I hoped that they would assist me one last time. This would be the second time that prosthetic arms would be introduced into my life. When I was only one year old I was given a set of prosthetic arms. My mother explained to me at the time that those arms were absolutely ludicrous. The arms were attached to a vest, but the apparatus weighed more than I did, and it was impossible for me to do anything with them. Mom told the doctors that if they did not get rid of this monstrosity she was going to throw it in the Ocean. We returned the arms and that was the end of them.

When I requested prosthetic arms in high school, Shriners hospital was totally on board with this and said that they would create a set for me. I explained to them that arms would be helpful in college because I could not carry a lunch tray otherwise, and I was thinking ahead to when I get older and perhaps would need to carry a baby. These were my reasons for desiring prostheses, and this is how I managed to continue receiving services at Shriners' Hospital for Children until my 21st birthday.

I think the orthopedic department was even more excited to work on making arms for me than I was to get them. This time the doctors were very conscious of the weight of the prostheses. They knew that I needed something that weighed very little, so that my legs did not collapse under me. Again I was fitted for a vest to which the arms were attached. The vest was made to be as lightweight as possible, and they attached the arms to it. There was a strap across my chest that kept the vest in place. I could manipulate a lever that would lock the arms either bent or straight. Then there were two little electronic circles that my fingers touched that made the hands open and shut. Both of these tasks were achieved by using my own hands inside the prostheses.

The process of obtaining "arms" was more fun than actually using them. When the arms were complete, I remember putting them on for the first time. They felt huge. When I looked at myself in the mirror I saw someone else. I had big shoulders and long arms coming off of my body for the first time in my life. When I tried to do things like opening a door or picking something up, it was difficult. The entire apparatus was heavy, even though they tried very hard to make it weigh as little as possible. I wore a shirt that would work with the arms, and the buttons were replaced with Velcro. I was married to Velcro yet again - a constant childhood reminder that I was different.

The reaction of my friends and family was interesting. I remember wearing the arms and having a conversation with my mom. She was telling me about a dream she had when I was a child. She prayed that some day her daughter would have arms. In that dream I had arms and I walked up to her and gave her a hug. That day she asked me for a hug and I looked at her and refused. I told her that these arms were not really a part of me... they were just an experiment and perhaps the dream of a hopeful mother. I took them off and gave her a hug.

My sister reacted with shock. I was in my room waiting excitedly for her to come home from work. I yelled from my room and told her to go into the hallway because I had something to show her. I walked out wearing my arms and she was clearly stunned. After that I showed her how the arms worked, it became a great topic of conversation for us.

The prosthetic arms did provide me with some interesting stories. One day I was taking the train to Worcester with my friend Katie. This was one of the first times that my friends would see my arms. I figured it would be easier to wear them than to have to carry them, because they were heavy. I had a disability rate on the train, but I did not actually carry a card because my disability was so visible, no one had ever questioned me until that day. I walked up to the counter with Katie and we asked for our tickets for the train. The teller quoted me the full price. I explained that I had a disability. He looked at me and asked if I had a card. I said that I did not. Then, without thinking, I pulled up my arms and dropped them onto the counter. The arms made a crashing sound as they hit the counter, and the teller's face went ashen. He quickly gave me my ticket. After the fact, I realized that there definitely could have been a better way of getting a discount for the train to Worcester. I did not mean to cause anyone discomfort, but it was true that the arms were fake. I am just a very matter-of-fact individual, so I just showed him the facts, because that's the easiest thing to do in life. We boarded the train and did not have any other mishaps with the arms. I remember that I noticed that not as many people as usual were staring at me. I guess these arms looked real enough to people when I was sitting, which felt kind of weird to me.

When we got to Worcester we met up with my friends and my boyfriend. I remember totally confusing one of our friends. That particular day I looked very different from my usual self. Not only did I have a set of arms, but I had just dyed my hair red. When my friend walked in the door my back was turned to her. I was sitting on my boyfriend's lap with red hair and arms and she did not even recognize me. Over the course of the next year, I used my arms very little. The one area in which I found the arms to be useful was teaching my disability awareness program. I brought my arms to work and that's where they stayed.

My arms are gone now, and I am not really sure where I left them. They were an experiment. I was independent before them, and they seemed to take that independence away. I cannot find a single photograph of me with my arms. That goes to show you how much I really did not like them.

Chapter 3
Perceptions of Life

Memories

Scattered memories are what is left of the painful years
Strength was necessary to prevail and that meant
leaving pieces behind
Barriers of strength were built all around to keep safe

No one knows the true impact their actions and
words have on another
Some actions gave me strength
Some words gave me hope

Other actions hurt me deep to the core
Other words brought me deep inside

That strength brought me to the other side;
never would I let that pain prevail
Acceptance I have for the painful times
They are a part of who I am today

I have often thought that I was lucky to be born in the late 1970's, because medical advances were increasing in momentous ways, and services for people with disabilities were expanding. Despite a growing medical and social awareness, during my childhood I had to endure society's pitying glances and gapes, and other people's belief that I would never be able to live a happy and fulfilling life. The medical treatment that I endured were numerous, including blood transfusions, long inpatient care, multiple surgeries, and occupational and physical therapy; however, the social stigma of disability felt worse. Overcoming my medical issues was easy compared to rising above the public's opinion of my abilities.

From a very young age, people would stare at me and/or feel pity for me. When I was a baby my mother would avoid people when we went for walks in the stroller. She found that they would be shocked by my appearance and would not know how to react. She would have to deal with their awkwardness and their inappropriate questions. From the age of about two and a half I understood that I was different, and for about as long as I have been able to talk I have helped people comprehend my difference. Unfortunately, neither adults nor children have always understood my message

From as far back as I can remember, people have stared at me, and not usually in a pleasant way. As an adult I learned to put staring into categories. Category one consists of young children who are very curious and just do not understand. This particular category enables me to use education as a tool to broaden a young child's experience. I do my best to talk about my disability and explain why I am different. Children are often shy with questions, so I pose questions myself. Sometimes I just wave or smile. They often do the same back. I no longer seem so scary to them.

Category two is adults or children who are old enough to ask questions and know that staring is impolite, but stare anyway. I find myself glaring back at these people. Of course I realize that two wrongs do not make a right, but historically it has been the best way for me to respond. Individuals in this category generally catch on quickly. The child or group of children see me and turn away. Sometimes they will turn back and try to stare a little more, and I repeat the same action. Their own discomfort makes them to stop. If individuals are in close enough proximity, I may try to engage them in conversation and tell them how rude they are being. My reaction in this case depends upon what the physical distance is between the person staring and myself.

Category three is composed of children or adults who stare with a look of disgust or unkindness of some sort. I find that this group also may use hand gestures. They might point or pull their hands into their shirts. Sometimes, they even laugh. This group, I approach directly. I tell them that what they are doing is rude and they need to stop. This is startling to them, but I really do not care. What they are doing is beyond ignorant, and I feel that it is important to call them on it. With any luck, the shock they feel at my reaction will give them a clue, and they might think before they repeat their behavior.

I have fewer memories of my childhood than most adults, and many of those memories are painful. I learned to build a high tolerance for pain and gain the ability to shut down my emotions. I was exposed to many harsh realities of life that no child should have to deal with while young. Recently, my mother shared that when I was about six years old I told her that I was happy that she kept me. It brought tears to both of our eyes when we thought about a child so young, yet able to understand a concept so complex. This profound understanding is the basis for my success as an adult.

When I was four years old, my mom discovered me looking in the mirror saying, "I love you.". Childhood innocence and acceptance is beautiful, but it does not stay with us forever. Growing up, I was not comfortable with my body. My entire life, people stared at me, making fun of me and pitying me. I remember a time at the local swimming pool when I was wrapped in a towel to get warm. I was talking to another kid and everything was fine until I removed my towel to go back into the pool. The child had not seen me before and had no idea that I had a disability, because the towel was so big. As soon as the towel came off I saw his face change to shock and fear. He quickly found a reason to leave. The experience was painful but not unusual. It was unusual, however, for my disability to go unnoticed at first and then became apparent. It did not take long before I started wondering if I really was okay or if I was weird, as other people said I was. My way of dealing with the staring, the pain and the mockery has changed through the years, as I have grown and matured. As a youth I realized that I could hide my pain with laughter, so when other children made fun of me I would laugh with them. This made them stop a lot faster than they would have if I cried. Laughter was not the response they anticipated. I found out quickly that humor puts a stop to things right away. The truth is that when people make fun of others, they are doing it so they can feel better about themselves. It has nothing to do with your difference, but rather, with their own issues. So when I would not cry in response to their cruelty, they stopped their behavior because I was not giving them the reaction they expected.

It was not easy being a child with a disability. I endured taunts and stares all the time, but I kept a smile on my face and moved forward. I understood very young that I was different, and for the most part I was usually comfortable with that difference. Sometimes I really did wish that I was physically similar to my friends. I remember being in second grade and wishing that I had arms, so at snack time I decided that my friends were going to help me reach that goal. I had a friend on either side of me. Both of them grabbed onto my hands and pulled their hardest until the teacher noticed and came over to us. They quickly let go of my hands and we started giggling, and since she did not actually understand what we were doing, she left us alone.

Sometimes the worst pain came from adults. I dealt with the ignorance of adults with my mother's time-honored catch phrases: "Sticks and stones may break my bones but names will never hurt me" and "I'm sorry that you have such a small mind". The first phrase was just a way to respond to adults and pretend they could not hurt me. In reality, I was hurting terribly inside, because words hurt more than physical pain. My second response took adults by surprise, but until I was older I never understood why. Think about it for a moment: a child of six looks up at an adult, and says, "I'm sorry you have such a small mind.". Then she turns around and walks away.

My surgeries were concentrated on my legs, but most of the denigration I experienced in my life was centered on my little hands. I was self-conscious growing up. I walked differently from others, and to make matters worse, I was one of the lucky ones who hit puberty before the other girls in my class. I added wearing a bra to all the other things that made me different

Growing up I wore a lot of baggy clothes, saying it was because of my leg braces. Even though as I aged, I no longer wore braces, I continued wearing the same kind of clothes. I was hiding. I did not want people to see my legs and my scars. I could not hide my hands but I could hide some things, and so I did.

It was not until I started dating that I became more aware of myself as an emerging woman. This transition began immediately after a boy showed interest in me. Shortly after our relationship ended I started caring about how I looked I realized that I was pretty and that there was no reason to hide behind all those loose-fitting clothes. I started shopping for new clothing that fit me. I remember so many of my friends thinking that I lost a lot of weight and saying that I looked great. It was also a time in my life that I began not to care what other people thought of me. No longer did I hide any part of myself. I wore shorts and showed my scars with pride. I bought the cute outfits all my friends were wearing and got many compliments.

I dealt with the pain of being different partly by simply forgetting about it. I still can't remember a great deal of my childhood, but there are still some memories that linger, both good and bad. In elementary school when I was exposed to teasing and the staring. At lunch, in the cafeteria with my friends, I remember looking up across the lunchroom and seeing two boys who were laughing and staring right at me I could not have been older than seven or eight. Then one of the boys pulled both of his arms into his shirt and just had his hands sticking out. The boy next to him pointed at him and laughed. I turned around and started talking with a friend and ignored him but this experience had an impact. It has been over 20 years and I still remember that day.

In the fifth grade, a couple of boys were making fun of me at recess, doing the usual laughing and pointing. Those boys were in for a surprise. Other boys in my class saw this happening to me and they did not approve. The next thing I knew, all of the boys in my fifth grade class went after the two of them. I never had a problem with those hecklers again.

I wish I could say that as I have gotten older I have dealt with less ignorance. I still get the stares and the pity, or even sometimes-random strangers coming up to me needing to help me. Often when I am at a store paying for items, one of the cashiers tries to put my credit card or receipt in my purse. It even happens that if I am a little slow getting my credit card out of my wallet, a cashier will grab my purse and try and start opening it for me. It blows my mind. I was raised with the idea that you never touch someone else's purse. I have never seen this happen to anybody without a disability.

When I was in graduate school. I was at the library and pulled out some NyQuil tablets and was trying to open them. Out of nowhere this guy walked right up to me and grabbed them out of my hands and said, "Let me help you.". I looked at the guy and said, "I do not know who you are. Please give me back my NyQuil.". I did realize that opening NyQuil tablets is a pain in the butt for most people. I would have welcomed the help had this individual just come over and asked me.

I spent a lot of time doing things just to prove people wrong. As I got older I began to look for opportunities to shock people. Here I am, a person with a disability who is very comfortable with my reality. Oddly enough, I see many people who are not disabled yet very uncomfortable in their own skin. Perhaps if we all became more comfortable within ourselves, the world can change.

Soon after I got my driver's license it occurred to me that I had a new way to freak out the world. One of the first things I wanted to do was go through a drive-through, to see how people would react. What would they say, how would they look at me, and what would they do? I understand that this was not the nicest thing that I might do. When you spend a lifetime dealing with ignorance, sometimes you just want to throw it back. So the very day I got my license, I went to a Wendy's drive-through . The worker was not really sure what to do about my no-arms, and it took me a minute to manage a drive-through. The worker had a shocked face. I put the car in park, and reached out the window. It took her a minute, but she figured it out. Like everyone else, I go through drive-through for convenience. Sometimes I get someone who is shocked and confused hot to help me, and other days, they are unfazed. A few have even come outside to give me my food.

 I remember one particular time when I shocked someone without even trying. I was driving with a friend, on our way to going to Friendly's. I went to turn left into the parking lot just as a woman was walking across to her car. I waved her on, but the look on her face was priceless. I am not sure if she noticed my hand or that I did not have arms. Her face went a little white and she just stood there and stared. After a second or two she gathered herself, and ran across the parking lot. We all had a good laugh and went to lunch.

They say that your childhood stays with you even when you become an adult. I agree. When I was student teaching, I experienced what is referred to as a trigger. There was a girl in class who had a disability. The other girls were not always nice to her. One particular day they crossed the line. They were laughing and being mean, pretending to make her part of the group while making fun of her. I saw her do exactly the same thing I did as a child: she laughed. The girls continued to tease her, but she quickly broke into tears. At that moment, something inside of me just snapped. I ran right up to those girls, extremely upset. I sent them all back downstairs and asked another teacher to watch them while I went into the back room. I kicked everything I could find. My fury increased when I realized that, I was watching my own childhood unfold, except, it was not happening to me. Once I collected myself I went back into the classroom, sat down with the girls and we had a long discussion. I posed this question to them: why do people sometimes laugh because it is funny, but other times laughter keeps the pain away. I also talked to them about what they had done. We spoke about their actions and how they were wrong and why. We talked about why I got so upset. This experience was a teaching moment, and definitely had an impact on them. They may not have become best friends with the girl, but they showed her more respect after that day.

Growing up was not easy. If anyone laughed, stared, or poked fun at me when my big sister Lisa was around, she made it stop fast. She would often use statements like: "Take a picture, it lasts longer,". Or "Stare a little longer and I'll make you permanently like her". Both comments would send kids running, and I could soldier on without being teased.

Over the years, my sister Lisa has continued to be my advocate. She puts people in their place when they ask an inappropriate question, or just flat-out tells them that are rude for staring. She is an advocate for people with disabilities. She has raised her son to accept people for who they are, and has never silenced his questions. I think Lisa's son Evan was about two and a half when he first noticed my difference, and he asked why I was using my feet to play with blocks. One time he got his hands stuck in his shirt and he commented that he looked like Aunt Sheila, and this was an awesome thing to him. Lisa has been great about answering his questions and creating an environment that supports difference. I remember my nephew being very confused about why people wanted to take pictures and videos of me and air them on television. He did not see anything that I did as special. I was simply his Aunt Sheila. As he has gotten older, he has met children with disabilities and he treats them the same as he would any other kid.

Recently Lisa, Evan, and I were at the mall and kids were staring at me. To be honest, I was busy having fun with my family and didn't even really notice them . Lisa did, however, and she asked me, "Are you over that?" I answered, "Yes, I am". She shrugged and said, "O.k., I guess I'll get over it, too". While it's true that the staring is happening still, for the most part I give it no notice. Sometimes I will see a child giving me a curious stare, and I go over and say hello. Or maybe if I am having a bad day, I will remind a person that it is rude to stare. Overall, I am sorry that people display ignorance instead of acceptance, because acceptance makes the world a much nicer place for all of us.

My first full sentence was, "Mommy, I can do that." That tells you a lot about my personality as a young child. You have guessed by now that asking for help is something I have never liked. This comes from being raised with the message that I could do things for myself. This was absolutely necessary, because if I didn't believe that I was capable of solving my own problems, I would not be the person I am today. I was a very determined little girl, continually figuring out how to meet challenges. My family always stood by me as I worked things out, and they gave me support as it was needed. Even when I really needed help, I still didn't like accepting it. Sometimes it made me feel that I had failed, and in my world failure was unacceptable. As I got older, life taught me that there are times when everyone needs to ask for help, and unfortunately, this was a difficult lesson for me to learn. There have been many times in my life that I brought myself to exhaustion before asking for help.

The other side of receiving help was wondering why someone would want to help me. Was it because they thought I was not capable of doing something on my own? As soon as that thought crossed my mind I was off to prove them wrong. Did they want to help me because they felt sorry for me? This kind of help was the most difficult for me, but often it is hard to tell the reasons someone might reach out to help me. I was a strong, independent person and I could do anything without aid, thank you very much.

As I have gotten older I have learned that assistance is a part of life. I understand now that receiving someone's assistance does not make you less than competent. If anything, it makes you stronger, because so many people are unable to ask for help but may really need it. When I was younger, I did not want to bother anybody. Now I don't worry so much about that. If I need help, I will ask, and if someone gives it to me, I am grateful. At this point in my life I have decided that the worst thing somebody can tell me is "no". I surround myself with people who are genuine and caring, so when I ask for help there are usually people willing to give it to me. Of course, there are many times when I need to ask random strangers to help me out. I have asked people in the grocery store to grab things from the top shelf. There is no need for me to try to jump up and down and knock things down on my own, but I get help on my own terms in a way that makes me feel independent.

Chapter 4
The Mirror

The Mirror

The mirror which is me
Adaptable, awesome, approachable
You see in me…
Bold, bubbly and bright in spirit.

The mirror which is me
Empowering reflection of dynamic drive
Strong, unstoppable determination
Fearless innovation…

The mirror which is me
Indomitable, excitable and unyielding
Undauntable inspirational force
Intrepid daring power

The mirror which is me
Mischievous, playful and free
Loving all that is thee
All of this you see in me

The mirror which is me
The mirror which is thee

*T*ake a moment to think about the role of sports in your life. Most of us have been involved with athletics, perhaps as a youth in gym class or a team sport, or even professionally, as an adult. For those with a disability, community sports can provide access to independence. Sports have the ability to expand the mind, body, and spirit when truly integrated into a person's life. As a person with a disability, I have observed this in my own life.

When I was a kid I had many hours of physical and orthopedic therapy in school. My therapist helped me learn so many different things, and even managed to make our time together fun. My therapist gave me a pair of Fisher-Price skates, which allowed me to keep wearing my sneakers. I put my foot into the skates and very slowly the therapist began to teach me how to roller-skate. It took a lot of effort at first, and balancing was pretty hard, but slowly I found I was able to skate down the hallway of my school. Once I mastered the art of roller-skating, I decided to bring my skates to Shriners' Hospital for Children and show Dr. Kruger how good I was!

I wanted to surprise Dr. Kruger, but I did show one of the nurses that I had a pair of roller skates with me. She asked me if I was going to ask Dr. Kruger if it was okay if I learned to roller skate. I said simply that today I was going to show him how I already am a decent skater. When my name was called to come to the clinic the nurse looked up at Dr. Kruger and said, "Sheila has a surprise to show you today, Dr. Kruger," and then I skated in, so proud of myself. Dr. Kruger jumped up from his seat, really concerned that I was going to fall. I told him not to worry, that I "had" this and that I already knew how to skate. Once I skated to him he calmed down a little bit. He proceeded to tell me that it was too dangerous for me to be roller-skating. He asked me what would happen if I fell. I told him I loved roller-skating, and although he tried for a few minutes to warn me about the dangers of skating, he soon realized he was fighting a losing battle.

Once I got really good at roller skating my mom put me in an after school program at a rink just around the corner from my house and enrolled me in lessons. One of the first things I learned to do was get myself up. My teacher was very creative. He got on the floor and put his arms behind his back to figure out how I would be able to get off the ground on my own. We agreed that the best way would be from a kneeling position. I would put one foot flat on the ground and then make a small hop in order to bring my other foot up to a flat position. This was not easy to accomplish, and we did it in steps. At first I was given a baton that I could put on the ground and use to push myself up, thus not needing to make that small hop. After I developed the strength and necessary balance, the baton was taken away and before I knew it, I could get off the floor without assistance.

I had so much fun roller-skating. My skating technique consisted of scissor skating, which was just bringing my legs in and out instead of back and forth, which was difficult for me to do with my body. I learned to skate backwards and I ultimately was able to do twists and turns. It was great fun and awesome to know that when my friends went out roller-skating, I could go, too. Skating was not the only activity that I enjoyed as a kid. Thanks to my cousin Stephen, I also played soccer.

When I was younger I spent a lot of time with my cousin Stephen, and it was not unusual for me to accompany him to one of his activities. That's how I began to play soccer. At first I just watched the practice, although after a while it was pretty boring. I don't remember how I convinced the coach to let me play with all the boys, but somehow I did, so I would go to soccer practice with Stephen and play right along with him and the team. It was fun, and eventually I became a pretty good player. I learned how to dribble, and before I knew it my kicks were getting stronger. When the season ended I convinced my mom to let me join my own soccer team.

I played soccer on a girls' team for about four years. It was a blast and it strengthened my whole body, especially my legs. This was the first time that I was involved in a team sport, and I was treated well. I tried every position, and the only time they had to change things around for me was when there was a throw-in. Let's face it, there was no way I was going to pick up a ball and throw it over my head. I got to try to be goalie once. That was something I will never forget, and something I will never try again. Why I thought it would be a good idea to try to play goalie with no arms is beyond me. I did, though, and the coach agreed to it. I decided that the best way to stop the ball would be with my head, and I did do that, but I also knocked myself unconscious, although only for a few seconds. If you don't have arms I do not recommend trying to be a soccer goalie!

As a kid I was known to mess with people a little bit. I figured that if people were going to make assumptions about me, then I would use those assumptions against them. People saw me as a little child with a disability and did not expect me to be any kind of a threat. I used these assumptions to help me when I was playing soccer. I would lay low and then steal the ball away, right before their eyes. I had no fear. I would rush right into people, stop and kick the ball out from underneath their legs. Eventually people learned to question their assumptions and I was treated equally, which is of course what I wanted from the start. Unbeknownst to me, the hours I spent playing soccer significantly strengthened my legs.

I realized how much soccer was making my legs stronger when I was in gym class. We played kickball and when it was my turn, the pitcher would come up close and roll the ball to me because I usually couldn't kick very far. I remember the day this changed, because it was such a thrill for me. As always, the pitcher moved closer but this time I kicked the ball so hard it went over his head and all the way to the back of the field! I was filled with happiness! After that, they stopped moving so close.

I learned to swim when I was very young through. a combination of private swim classes and lessons with my dad. This was not easy for me to grasp. Once I did, however, I loved it! I had two types of floating devices because I could not use Swimmies with no arms. At first the instructors tried to put me in a little life vest. This was very uncomfortable, sliding up around my neck so I felt that I couldn't breathe. Then they tried a bubble. This was a Styrofoam oval that strapped around my stomach. It allowed me to float around in the water and feel safe, while still breathing easily. When I first started using the bubble I would do a face-plant in the water, but it didn't take long before my dad removed the bubble and taught me to swim the same way he had done with my sisters.

Dad taught me to float, and then as I got more comfortable, I kicked my feet to move around. Swimming on top of the water seemed so difficult to me because I always felt as though I was falling into the water face down. Today I am comfortable swimming. I do not know how to do specific strokes, but I can swim back and forth in a pool and go underwater without any fear. As a child, my mom used to tell me I was a little fish, since you would find me in the pool on most summer days. One reason for this was that when it was hot out, being in the pool felt better. The other motivation was that the water made my legs feel good. There was no pressure on my knees and I could swim for hours, keeping up with the other kids. I didn't need to wear my leg braces in the water, and that was definitely a huge plus when I was swimming. As I got older and did not need an adult with me at the pool, I stopped wearing one-piece bathing suits because it was really difficult for me to get them on and off by myself.

Every summer my family went camping. The Boston Minuteman Campground of Littleton, Massachusetts was like a second home to me. We spent most summers there because my dad worked at the campground part-time, and I always felt welcome and safe. At the campground, Joy the Magical Clown came every holiday weekend to perform magic tricks for the kids and also happened to be a close friend of my family. As a child I only asked him for one thing, and that was to find a magic trick that I could do. This was not an easy task, but he was up to the challenge, and it was a challenge that he met not once, but twice. These days, he is waiting for me to come to clown school so I can learn more. He is a person in my life who has always made sure that I was included in the fun. I have memories of him pulling me around the campground in my little red wagon, just before the magic show started.

My mode of transportations as a child was my mini/Big Wheel, which allowed me to keep up with my friends. I was able to go as fast as the wind and it was always such an amazing feeling. I loved the speed and was often found barreling down a hill at our local campground. The hill seemed huge to me, because I was so little. I would take my feet off the pedals and fly down the hill. This was not particularly safe, because sometimes I would bump into a tree or fly off the bike, but I continued to do it again and again because it was so much fun.

As I got older I traded in my mini-wheel for a Big Wheel. I probably had about three different ones, and they continued to be my mode of transportation for a long time. I still remember the day that the last big-wheel fell apart. It was a "crest" bike that looked just like the Crest toothpaste tube. It was blue, red and white. My mother saved box tops to get it sent to us in the mail. I was riding around the campground with my friends when I heard a crack and a pop, and all of a sudden I was on the ground. The bike had fallen into three pieces. I got off the ground and grabbed one piece of the bike, and my two friends each took one piece. We walked it back to my family's campsite in search of my dad. When I found him, I said, "Dad, it is broken can you fix it, please?" It was a sad day for my dad when he had to tell me "no," He said, "I can not fix your bike, Sheila. It is plastic and it is cracked and there is nothing I can do".

That was the last Big Wheel I owned. It would be about five years before my parents tried to help me ride another kind of bike. Learning to ride my first two-wheeler bike was really exciting and difficult. My dad lengthened the handlebars by welding on additional metal, to give them the reach I needed. He also bent them closer, for easy access. Riding the bike safely and learning to balance on two wheels was a completely different story. When I first started riding the bike it had training wheels, as it does for most kids. For some reason I just never could get the balance, and tipped over a number of times. My parents wanted me to wear a helmet, as they were worried about my safety. I never liked wearing a helmet. To this day, my parents and I remember the story differently. I was completely against putting on the helmet, and then finally deciding, "Fine I'll do it!" because I wanted to learn to ride a bike. My parents remember me being a teenager and wanting nothing to do with the helmet, and refusing to wear it, no matter what. They felt it was important enough that they put away the bike. At some point the bike was gone and I never got to ride it again.

Years went by and occasionally I would think about looking for a bicycle. Twice, I got serious about buying one, but each time I would end up buying a car instead. Once I owned a car I never had the funds to purchase a bicycle. I was trying to find a bike online, so I was unable to try it out. I did not want just to buy something and hope for the best, especially since bicycles are so expensive. I dropped idea until the summer of 2012. I found a place in New Hampshire, an hour's ride from my house where I could try test-driving a bicycle. Northeast Passage, a program at the University of New Hampshire that offers adaptive sports, was where I finally found my bike. The same group also introduced me to an adaptive sports program ten minutes from my house. In September I enrolled in Spaulding Hospital's Adaptive Sports Program in Salem, Massachusetts. They had several cycling clinics that gave me the opportunity to test drive the banana peel bike. Trailmate manufactures the bike. It is a one-piece recumbent tricycle. It has foot brakes and the steering is done with your hips. It is a natural fit for me, and so easy to maneuver that I fell in love with it.

After the first clinic I bought my own bike, although it was mid-fall, so I only had a short time before winter arrived and I had to put it away. Over the winter I planned to figure out how to transport my bike easily, and I am now looking into adding a gear to it as well. I am excited that after almost 15 years I now can ride a bike all on my own. Though biking was only one of my many interesting childhood activities.

One hot summer day when I was about 10 years old, my dad noticed that I seemed really bored, so he suggested that I find something to do. I looked at him and said, "I want to go horseback riding." He shrugged his shoulders and said, "O.k., let's find a place." We looked through the yellow pages (no Google then!). We quickly found a place to go trail riding, and we were there within an hour. When we phoned to make the arrangements, we forgot to tell them one small detail about me. That's right: the disability piece. Oops! When we arrived they were a little shocked and were unsure if I would be able to ride. My dad said I would be fine and told them that we did these kinds of things all the time. He signed the release form and we began to figure out how riding with no arms would work. Getting on the horse was a bit difficult, and I needed the help of two people. Once I was on, the next problem was how to steer the horse. We were riding Western style and steering only required one hand, but the reins were short. One of the staff suggested that we just extend the reins by tying the two together, so I could reach. The steering was not perfect, but there was someone walking with me, so it was fine. We had a great trail ride through the forest and I knew this was something that I wanted to do again.

At the start of high school I was all about soccer, until I realized how much running was involved. When I stopped soccer, I realized I needed something new, and decided it was time to learn to ride a horse properly. This time Mom and I went through the Yellow Pages. We found a place in North Andover, Massachusetts, called Ironstone Farm. We called, had a great conversation about their program, and set up an appointment. As we hung up we realized that once again we forgot to tell them that I had a disability. We knew they had a program for people with disabilities, so we didn't think it would be a problem. We called back to let them know that small detail about me. I think they found it weird that we forgot to let them know about my situation, but nonetheless, I signed up.

I spent the next four years taking horseback riding lessons. We rode English style so the steering was a little easier, and we kept the long reins idea from my first trail ride. I learned how to groom a horse and how to ride. Most of my lessons were private, but took some with my sister, Christine. One of the most difficult techniques for me to master was the half-seat position. Most people have the option of putting their hands down to hold themselves in position. Once I mastered half- seat, I was solid on the horse, and I was proud. I went on to learn how to steer a horse without the reins, which was very helpful. On occasion the horse would pull his head down, and I would lose my grip on the reins. When this happened I used my legs to go in a particular direction. I just had to squeeze my legs in the opposite way and would bring the horse to a stop by squeezing with both legs.

I never learned to gallop, but I did learn to canter, although the very first time, it happened by accident. My sister Christine and I were trotting around the ring as usual, and our teacher decided that we should try some short cross jumps, which means actually jumping over a barrier. My parents had come to watch the lesson that day and it was Dad's first time seeing me ride in a long time. We had the cross jumps setup and had trotted through once or twice already. It was my turn again, and I gave the horse a big kick before I realized that the animal was going really fast… faster than ever before. I screamed to my teacher and she told me to hold my seat and I would be fine. The horse then jumped the cross jump to the far right, which was a bit high for me. When I went over it was as scary as anything I had ever done, and the most exciting feeling ever. When I landed I caught my breath and asked what had just happened. My teacher explained that I had kicked the horse just right and thrown him into a canter. I immediately asked if we could do it again. It was probably not the best lesson for Dad to observe, watching his daughter as she as she flew on a horse all by myself!

Some time later, Dad and I went riding with a friend who owned horses and I was on Oreo and my dad was on the Clydesdale, which was huge. He could not get on or off the horse without help. As we began to ride, my horse got spooked and my Dad was again in the position of watching me on a horse, wondering if I was going to fall and not being able to do anything about it. The horse was spooked and tried to throw me, and almost succeeded. I managed to hold on by an ankle, literally, as I tucked it around the horse's neck while I was falling to the left. I grabbed on with my ankle and this gave our friend just enough time to take hold of the horse and push me back up. Now that I was ready for this horse, we went on our ride, and the next few times he tried to throw me off I was as solid as a rock. After we finished our ride we noticed a storm was coming in, and which is why Oreo had been spooked.

As much as I enjoyed physical activities as a child, I was also interested in babysitting. As the youngest child of three I cannot say I had a lot of experience with babies. I did have a kid sister doll. I brushed her hair, changed her clothes, and carried her around. I also had other dolls that had diapers, and I always made sure they were clean. I did all of this with my feet. Of course, I was aware of my limits with real babies,. I was comfortable holding a baby as long as I was sitting with the baby in the crook of my knee. I was at ease picking up babies if they were past six months old, because by then they had good control of their heads and could hold on if necessary. When I was 12 years old I was presented with the opportunity to become a babysitter. I had babysat with one of my friends for a family just down the street from my house, and they had a need for a sitter.

The family had two children. Their older was about three years old and the younger, a little over six months. I had a very open conversation with the woman about my abilities. I felt it was important to be upfront and honest if I was going to take care of her children. I explained to her that I was fully capable of changing the baby's clothing and diaper. I told her my biggest concern was the crib. I explained that taking the child in and out of the crib made me nervous, because reaching in would be extremely difficult. She felt that it was fine for the baby to take her naps on a blanket downstairs with me. Her biggest worry was that if there was an emergency, would I be able to pick up the baby to get outside. I explained to her that I did not see this as a concern because I could carry the child if needed.

Before I knew it, I was a babysitter. I remember the first time I changed a diaper. It was pretty easy. I did with my feet, just the way I had with all my dolls. This time, though, it was the real thing. As the years went on there were different challenges that I met as a babysitter. I learned to take the baby in and out of the crib, because as she got older we found that all she needed to do was wrap her arms around my neck and I would pick her up and put her down. The same method worked for the highchair. As the older sister grew, she questioned how I would change her sister's diaper. One day she told me that I was doing it wrong. She said her mom used her hands and I used my feet. She was trying to explain to me that diapering was not to be done with one's feet. This led to a discussion about how I was a little different and I had to do things differently. She accepted this easily and came to the conclusion that I did things "way cooler"! I found out one day that grilled cheese was her favorite food. I applied creative thinking to this challenge. How I was going to make this happen? I put the toast in the toaster and then had to climb up on the countertop to turn the stove on with my toes. Then I jumped back down to the ground to put the toast and cheese in the frying pan, and heated them all together. It was not long before she declared that I made the best grilled cheese ever.

As I age, my passion to seek new adventure has not waned. Throughout my life, my sisters and I created crazy schemes to make sure all their activities included me. When I moved back east from graduate school I stayed with my sister, Lisa, and her husband, Mike. It was nice to have a place to crash while I looked for a job and an apartment. They live in New Hampshire and are big fans of four wheeling. I had been four wheeling a few times, but always seated in front of the driver. This time, it was Derby Weekend, and time to go ice fishing. It was cold when we bundled up to go out to the four-wheeler. Even though I had never ridden the four-wheeler with Lisa, it never crossed our minds that it would be a problem. Once we looked over the situation we realized that holding on with mittens was going to be a problem. Lisa's first thought was that we would put the hard case on the back so I would be able sit back against it, and I then figured that I could hold on with my legs the way I hold on to a horse.

This worked at first, but as we went faster I started bouncing around, and it felt like I was going to fall off. We stopped to re-adjust, as the hard case was not staying on correctly. That was when I said I wished I had something to go over my lap like a seatbelt, to help me feel safer. Lisa looked around and found a bungee cord. We both thought this was a great idea and proceeded to use it as a lap belt. I felt secure, so we took off on the four-wheeler on the trails of New Hampshire. It was so much fun to ride in the wind. An officer who made us aware of thin ice as we crossed on to the frozen lake stopped us once. He gave us a small-confused look for a second, but that was all.

Once we arrived at our destination we surprised a number of people, I guess they did not expect me to ride the four-wheeler with Lisa. Then they noticed the bungee lap belt and thought we were both crazy. My brother-in-law was very uncomfortable about what would happen if the bike flipped over. He thought I could have been killed. I knew the danger of riding a four-wheeler in the first place, and realized that the bungee cord could have made it a bit more dangerous. The reality for Lisa and me was that we needed a solution for me to ride, and this worked for us. This was not the first time I was belted into something so I could be included and it would not be the last. My brother-in-law, Mike, just did not understand that this was normal behavior for Lisa and I. It was nice that he was so concerned for my safety. At the end of the night he put me in the front of his four-wheeler and drove me over to the parking lot, where I caught a car ride home. Later, Lisa and I related the story to our mom, and she thought it was great that we figured out a way for me to ride on the four-wheel vehicle. We told her how some people the bungee cord was a bad idea, but she just shrugged and said, "How else were you going to stay on?" With a mother who has this attitude, it is no wonder that my sisters and I continue to be creative and inclusive in finding ways for us to have fun together.

One of the most dangerous and interesting exercise activity in which I have involved myself is fire spinning. I first got interested in spinning fire at a drumming dancing event. The event was indoors, and therefore there was no actual fire, but people were spinning with LED lights. I remember watching and thinking that it was amazing and looked like so much fun. Later that night I went over to one of the spinners and ask her where I could learn to do this. I was told that I needed to come to Wildfire. The first Wildfire event I attended involved more watching than participating. I watched the fire spinners and thought about how someday I could do it myself. I went to workshops and I learned about belly dancing and other things that were involved in the fire spinning community, and I decided I would come back again. A critical experience for me was the fact that for the entire weekend that I was at Wildfire there were no questions about whether I could do it or why I was there. It was a weekend of full acceptance, which was a reassuring experience since this has not always been the case. My first experiences of spinning fire happened because my boyfriend at the time saw how much I enjoyed watching everybody else spinning and worked on a way for me to do it myself.

He created a lengthening device that would allow me to spin the poi that many of my friends spun. Poi is a style of performance art that takes place at Wildfire. The equipment used for engaging in poi varies from a string to a chain that is tethered with a weight. In our case we used Kevlar wicking at the end to light the implement on fire. Then he took the contact juggling balls that we used and attached them, instead of the traditional poi, because he thought that it might be a little safer for me. These juggling balls had a Kevlar wicking set inside of a caged sphere. The juggling balls made things a little heavier for me, and the flame was not as bright or large as some of my friends' when I spun, but this was the first step towards being able to stand on the field with everyone and spin. It was a rush!. This original construction really got my brain cooking, thinking about how I could create something lighter and easier and would not spin in a such a way that there was danger the flame could come back at me.

I continued to watch my friends spin, and realized that I could make fire fans with this same device. A fire fan is a fan, typically constructed out of welded metal and Kevlar wicking. I knew it would be possible for me to do this. I remember how exciting it was when I finally solved the problem. I needed some aluminum poles and also a few other pieces of metal. I figured I would need some kind of saw, and maybe some screws and nuts. Then I also would need some wick and the assistance of at least one of my friends who was involved with toy making, for fire performance. Before I decided to go out and buy the supplies, I thought about it and realized that maybe some of this was over my head, so I decided to call my dad. I wanted to see what he thought about my construction ideas, because most of my life my father has made devices to allow me to be able to do what everyone else was doing.

My dad knew about some of the performances with fire that I had already done, and I was not sure how he was going to react when I told him I wanted to make yet another toy to allow me to dance with fire. I decided

I would approach him anyway and see what happened. I was pleasantly surprised when I told him what I wanted to do and he sat down right away to help me figure out how to make sure that I was safe. He and I went to the store and put the device together. As always, it was enjoyable to work side by side with my dad. Once we finished the construction I had the wicks attached, and before I knew it I was ready to spin with my new fire fan.

I recall a really interesting conversation with my sister while I was working with my dad to put that fire fan together. She told me that had she talked to Dad and he was a little concerned about what I was going to do. He felt that if he was involved with the making of this fire fan that it would at least be put together well. He knew that when I got something in my head that I want, I would do it, regardless of the challenges and potential consequences. He decided to help me to ensure it was made in the safest way possible. He was really cool about it and supported me even though he did not agree with what I was doing. He realized that this was my choice as an adult, and he wanted only to make it as safe as he could. Within a short period of time this modified fire fan was created, and I was able to go with my friends and dance with the fan that we made together, in a way that made me feel safe, yet it still had that flash of flame and excitement.

As with most fire performances, when you have a new toy it's great and you love it. Eventually, like everything else, all the other toys around you seem more interesting. I was also learning the long staff in martial arts. I worked hard in weapons class, learning different tricks. Many of my friends were doing staff work in martial arts. I found ways to move smoothly with the staff, and I was getting better and faster. I started watching and wondering if I could do my martial arts work with fire. One of the biggest concerns with the fire long staff was that whenever I tried to pick up one of my friends' staffs they felt too heavy. My martial arts staff was lightweight. One night at a friend's birthday party I noticed that someone had a double staff. Each staff was shorter and lighter. I didn't see why I couldn't simply use one of the staffs and be able to perform the moves that the rest of my friends were learning. I asked my friend, who had double staffs if I could use one staff to spin fire, and she said to feel free, and let her know when I was ready, and she would grab it for me. I had never done it before with fire, but I had been practicing in martial arts and I thought I that could do it. I checked in with the fire safeties, which included a person with a towel, who watches you while you spin, in case you catch fire. The fire safety is responsible for putting out the flame if you cannot do it yourself.

I was thrilled to try fire spinning with a staff. We decided that for safety reasons, one of the other staffers would spend the fuel off for me and I would continue from that point. In order to light the Kevlar wicking at the end of the staff you need first to dip it in white gas fuel. To avoid the fuel spitting at others while performing, it is necessary to spin off or shake off the extra fuel. I had a blast. The staff was a little short so I had to be more cautious, but it was amazing, and I was able to do all of the things I did with the martial arts staff. When I got more comfortable with it and the flame went down just a little bit, I lay down on the ground and started using my feet, the way I had seen some of my friends work with the staff for years.

I knew that this was something that I wanted to continue to do, so the same friend who had helped me make the fire fan created a staff for me that was lighter and longer and as safe as possible. It's been years now since my friend made that fire staff, and it has worked out really well. My martial arts training has allowed me to become proficient with the fire staff, and I have gotten faster and better. I do not spin as often as I used to, but I still use the fire staff when there are opportunities to spin fire, and I am more than happy to jump up and be a part of the fun.

Chapter 5
Advocating through Ignorance

Recognize

Look around and see that everything works for you
and nothing for me.

Life's basic rights are often denied to me and you never see.

Your structures make assumptions about how another must function

Why isn't it possible for you to entertain another way?

It would cost you nothing to give me equal footing

Yet you hold back and complicate the way.

If that is your position, then step back. Get out of the way.

I will find the solution as I always must.

Bending parts, keeping parts and splitting parts, and knew

Life's basic rights… they are for the many not the few.

Recognize you will.

Stand beside you must.

Change is coming through.

It is a must.

*M*y parents were my first advocates, and through their example I learned to be my own advocate. The need for self-advocacy arises frequently in my life. Situations in which I need to advocate for myself are innumerable, but include interactions with medical professionals, schools, colleges or work, social settings many more. It has not always been easy, though each time I became stronger for the experience. As an adult I'm not only my own self-advocate, but I've learned the importance of standing up for others. I was lucky to be given the tools to succeed and live an independent, fulfilling life. In my opinion, with that comes the responsibility to advocate for those who cannot advocate for themselves.

I was lucky to have Shriners Hospital for Children caring for me. There was only one incident where I can remember a doctor was unprofessional in his treatment. I woke up one morning and my ankle was swollen. I was unable to walk on it, and my mother said we needed to get it checked. At that point in my life I had been refusing to see my primary care doctor because he was male and I was a pre-teen female. I was growing up and could not handle having a male doctor, and my mom had not yet found me a new primary care physician. We ended up going to a clinic. This turned out to be a big mistake, as the doctor was rather confused and appeared to be quite concerned about the situation. He asked many questions about my medical history and in the end he said he would not be able to help us. He believed it was necessary for me to see my orthopedic surgeon in Springfield. This was for a swollen ankle. He refused to give us any care, even a simple X-ray of my ankle. We ended up driving two and a half hours to Shriners for them to look at my ankle to determine that I had sprained it. They put me in a cast and sent me home with crutches. I was glad to have Shriners Hospital for Children there to support me, but the day would come when I could no longer use their services, which worried me.

When I turned 21 I had to leave the care of Shriners, and that meant that I had to find a doctor familiar with my disability. Because my condition is rare, I have often had to fill in the details, which has often been difficult and irritating. When I left Shriners Hospital for Children, I was told to find a doctor for my orthopedic needs, just in case. It took me a few years to follow their advice, and that was when I realized that I needed to advocate more for myself, especially with medical personnel.

When I finally got around to finding an orthopedist, he treated me rudely. The doctor who examined me performed all the courses of action that I was used to from being a child at the clinic at Shriners. But once he started to speak it was nothing like Shriners. He seemed annoyed that I was coming to him without any acute issues, and did not seem to understand why I would want to have a doctor just in case I needed anything for my knee. I left thinking that it was a big waste of time and I didn't plan to have a "just in case" visit to a doctor for a long time.

I have encountered discrimination frequently throughout my life, as well as a significant amount of ignorance. I remember one summer when my family took a trip to the Museum of Science in Boston. We were going to see the Ramses exhibit. I was really excited, as I was very interested in the history of the world. Ancient Egypt was a topic I had studied in school. This particular exhibit had a gigantic amount of security around it, which was understandable. They had brought Ramses' tomb to the United States, along with many Egyptian artifacts. It was summertime, so I had on shorts and was wearing my long leg braces. We knew we were in for an extended day, and I wanted to be able to stay on my feet in order to see everything. Upon entering the exhibit we passed through a metal detector, and to no one in my family's surprise, the metal detector went off when I walked through the turnstile. But what happened next was surprising. The security guards pulled me aside, and called the supervisor. Let me remind you that I was a little kid of eight or nine years old wearing shorts and a pair of long metal braces. What did they think was going to happen when I went through the metal detector? Eventually, their supervisor came, and when she saw a child in shorts and braces, she dismissed the whole thing. I feel that it's important to remember that this was a situation that could have been very different had the guards simply recognized and acted upon the fact that I was a child, and posed no threat. Now I can understand the need for security because who knows what people are capable of doing, but I was a little kid with a disability being treated like a criminal.

I have faced discrimination in my daily life and although my intimate community accepted me, the world did not. This was brought home to me especially as I applied for jobs and no one ever called back. When I passed in my job applications, the expression on the faces of those I met assured me that the application would go no further. Finally, in my junior year I applied for a job at a local movie theater. I was granted an interview with an open-minded manager. During the interview she expressed her concern about my ability to be a cashier. I told her I would not have applied for the job if I didn't think I could do it, and suggested that she give me a chance. We went downstairs to the registers and I was able to show her that I could handle the job. She hired me with the contingency that we would try it out for a few weeks. Looking back, her actions seem discriminatory because her hesitation in hiring me was solely based on my disability. In truth, the only accommodation I needed was a stool to sit on, because standing all day was too difficult. Getting this job was my first step toward independence

From the moment I understand the meaning of the word "college", I knew I wanted to go. I went to a college prep high school, so a university education was the next logical step. When I was in my junior year I applied to colleges along with my friends. For the most part, my search for the right school paralleled theirs. I filled out the applications, wrote the college essays, and got recommendations. As time went on, I began to visit schools to see if they would work for me, and to decide if I was interested in their programs. One day I received a disturbing phone call from one of the colleges that had received my application. The school representative told me that they wanted me to come to the school to be sure that I could take care of my own personal needs if they were to accept me as a student.

I kept very calm as I spoke to the person on the phone. I said, "It is my understanding that as long as I come to your college and show you that I can take care of myself, you will accept me." I made it very clear that I wanted to have this in writing. If I made a trip to this place, I wanted some assurance that I would be accepted. The truth was that I was aware the phone call qualified as discrimination. There is no way they should ask me to prove my capabilities for personal care as a requirement for acceptance. I wanted it in writing so that I could bring it to an attorney if the need arose. My parents heard my side of the conversation. My father suggested that we wait for the letter and then take it to an attorney, and proceed from there.

We reviewed the letter when it arrived, and agreed that it would not help in proving the discriminatory nature of the phone call although my father brought it to the attorney just in case. They, however, came to the same conclusion, and we were unable to bring a suit against the college. I showed the letter to the guidance counselor at my high school, and the school was mortified, stating that they would remove this college from the list of recommended schools. I don't know if this actually happened, but I did feel supported by my school, which was important to me.

Attending college introduced me to world of opportunity and independence, along with some harsh realities. I had to advocate for myself at school to receive reasonable accommodations. They mirrored what I had had in high school, but it took some time before everything was arranged. The only procedural piece I had in preparation for the colleges was the documentation that I had a disability, as defined by the Americans with Disability Act. Halfway through my senior year of high school I had received many acceptances. I made my pick and was going to be a freshman at Suffolk University in the fall. It was an exciting time in my life. I had always wanted to go to college, and now it was really happening!

Before the fall semester began, there were a few things I needed to put in place that most students never have to worry about. I needed to go to Disability Services and identify myself as a student with a disability. I also had to make sure that Resident Life knew that I had a disability and what accommodations would be necessary for me. In the dorm, I was assigned to a room with only one roommate, even though the room usually held four students. I also requested a stepladder so that I would be able to reach things in my closet.

At every step, I had to educate those around me, and request the essential adjustments for my disability. My classrooms needs required a second set of books, and since it was an expense for the college, they were initially taken aback. I explained to them that my high school and middle school had provided me with this assistance and after a week or so, I had a second set of books. My next challenge was transporting my books to each classroom. Disability Services provided me with a locker outside of my classrooms, which gave me easy access to the books I needed for class. Finally, I needed a note taker. The school suggested that I speak to each course professor and find a student in the class who would allow me to photocopy his or her notes. This was recommended because they found that students took better notes than a non-student who attended the class just for this reason. I tried this when classes started, and it worked well for me.

The other accommodation new for me was a special chair, since leaning over for an extended period of time hurt my back, and it was decided that there was a need to find a sitting position that would work better for me. Welcome to my world. They tried to rig a higher chair and table so I would not have to bend over. The idea was nice, but like so many ideas in my youth, it made me stand out even more. I thanked the "inventor" and let him know that I would rather use the same chair and table as the other students. As the four years of college passed I noticed this chair and table in various classrooms, and was always grateful that I had chosen not to use it.

I have spent most of my life dealing with the ignorance and fear of others, and in response have continually chosen to educate people about my abilities. While working at Girls Inc. in Worcester, Massachusetts, I was presented with a great opportunity. The possibility arose to write a grant to fund an education program for the participants of Girls, Inc., and I was aware that this was an opportunity to develop a disability awareness program. My own personal experiences had taught me countless times that disability awareness is critical in both public schools and after-school programs.

On my very first day of work my mere presence caused a child to burst into tears and cry hysterically. She had never seen a person with a disability, and was terrified. One of the staff members calmed her down. I quickly stepped inside of one of the offices, so as not to further frighten her. Once the child recovered, I approached her and introduced myself. I encouraged her to ask questions, and after a few minutes she was all right.

All of the staff was incredibly supportive as I put the program together. In particular there was a woman named Dolores, for whose support I am still thankful. I had never created a program like this before, and it was a little intimidating. Dolores' support kept me going every day. Her help made the program happen, and I saw her as my partner. Over the next two months I worked hard, and knew it was important to involve as many community partners as possible. Shriners Hospital for Children, the Massachusetts Commission for the Blind, the Massachusetts Commission for the Deaf and Hard of Hearing and other local disability awareness programs agreed to collaborate. The curriculum was varied. I had guest speakers, interactive exercises, videos, handouts, games and songs. The girls learned about adaptive technology, independence for people with disabilities, sign language, and so on, and gained a deeper respect for and understanding of people with disabilities.

Once the program was running it was held twice a week. The program was a huge success. Staff would attend on a regular basis, as they were interested in the guest speakers and all the activities. At the end of the school year the entire school used sign language to present a song to their parents. I was extremely proud of the success of the program. A few months later I had the opportunity to rewrite the grant in an effort to become a national program for Girls Inc. We came in second place, losing to a sports program. It may not have been nationally recognized but I feel that I succeeded in the program locally, and coming in second was a huge accomplishment.

Inaccessibility is something that I have to deal with every day. As I have grown older I have noticed this more and more, and have learned that I have to be my own advocate every single day. I first started working for Girls Inc. just after my 21st birthday. I was incredibly excited about this opportunity, as it was my first professional job. The group was great at providing me with accessibility accommodations in the building. The classroom I worked in was terrific, as it was meant for children, which meant that most of the furnishings were low.

I remember one particular time I was immensely affected by inaccessibility. In order to get to work I had to take at least two buses from my house. If I was coming from school I had to walk down a hill to take the commuter rail, and then take two buses. Let's just say the day I got to drive to work was very exciting. One cold and rainy day I got to work a little early. The door was locked. I didn't have a key to the building. I tried banging on the door because I could see some lights and figured somebody was inside. Unfortunately, whoever was there could not hear me. I finally found a doorbell, but it was in the most inaccessible place you could imagine. It was about 7 feet in the air, about 3 feet over my head. There were no benches outside the building, either, so I sat on the cold pavement under a small shelter, trying not to get wet until someone either came outside and noticed me, or came to work.

These were daily realities for me and I learned to roll with them from a young age. I have come to realize that many of the inaccessible situations happened out of ignorance and were not meant to cause me pain. Nevertheless, the impact has been hurtful to many others, and me, which is why I continue to educate. Education has always been very important to me. From a young age I had planned to go to college, and after completing an undergraduate degree I realized that a graduate degree was necessary to continue with my employment goals. Little did I know at the time that graduate school would impact my advocacy goals enormously. It would also assist me in becoming even more independent.

As I searched for graduate programs I found myself looking everywhere in the United States, but I did have some criteria: no earthquakes, floods, tornadoes, or wildfires. These were some of the natural disasters that scared me. I explored all programs at each school because I was not 100% sure about counseling rehabilitation. I remember my mom asking me to stay on this side of the Mississippi River, please, and I said, "No problem, Mom, I can do that." Then I found a school in Arizona with a degree in criminal justice.

I remember talking to one of my ex-boyfriends about my concerns regarding moving to Arizona for graduate school. I had a list of reasons why I could not make this move, but every time I mentioned one of them to him he found a way to discount it. What it boiled down to was that I was afraid to move 3,000 miles away from everyone I knew. Once I realized it was only fear that was holding me back, I was all for doing it. Northern Arizona University in Flagstaff was the only school to which I applied. I had always wanted to go out West, and what better reason could there be than for graduate school?

Planning for and moving to Arizona was something I did pretty much on my own. I found an apartment online that seemed as though it would be pretty accessible. That was exciting. I was working a second job at Wal-Mart, and I was told that the job would transfer to Arizona. About a month or two before I was to leave, I finally got an acceptance notice from the college. I did have a bit of a meltdown just before I left, but continued to feel strongly about going to Arizona.

As with many things in life, there were a lot of mishaps on my path to Arizona. My kitty refused to get in the cat carrier the day we were leaving, so I had to leave her behind. When we arrived in Arizona my car was not there as planned, but it did arrive a day later. All my belongings arrived two weeks late, and the job that I thought was transferring from Massachusetts was a nightmare. When I spoke with the Wal-Mart managers in Flagstaff they had not heard anything about my being transferred. I went down to the security office to check into getting disability benefits, which was something that I really did not want in my life, but I was running out of options and needed income. Receiving disability benefits has been a struggle for me, partly because of all the negativity and judgment from others. Those opinions have been negative and degrading. As I have gotten older I realize that judgment will come from the privileged, no matter what. When you are receiving benefits, you are considered lazy and useless. If you have a job, people are shocked.

The first couple of months in Arizona were difficult. There were tears and lonely nights. While I was on the phone with my dad, he said, "If you want to come home, just say the word." As hard as it was, I knew I needed to stick it out at least until September. I went to Arizona to go to graduate school and I was not going to leave until I had at least made an attempt at it. As time went on things got better, as they usually do. I did get the job at Wal-Mart, and as it turned out, I got to remain on the Massachusetts pay scale, so I earned a lot more than I would have normally been paid in Arizona. I started to meet some people, and before I knew it school had started.

Moving to Arizona was one of the hardest things I have ever done. It was also one of the best. I got to find out who I truly was and what I wanted in my life. I was 3000 miles from anyone I knew, and got to try everything and be anyone I wanted to be, without question or judgment. I changed a great deal in graduate school, and I really think it was for the better. I found the kind of independence I never had. I also found respect and gratitude for what had always been given to me. In a manner of speaking, I grew up in Arizona, as my Mom was not around the corner to fix the little things she always had. I became a stronger advocate for myself, dealing with discrimination, and in general became a stronger, more confident woman.

Nothing is without its bumps in the road, and just when I thought things were going well, I tried to transfer my driver's license. Chaos ensued. First there was a long waiting line, naturally. Then there was confusion as to what restrictions should be indicated on my license, and so a call was made to the medical review board for advice. In less then five minutes a woman who knew nothing about my driving background or me deemed it necessary for me to take and successfully complete a road test and possibly a medical evaluation. The representative looked at me and told me that because I drove with my feet I needed to take a road test. I refused, and asked what my options were for an appeal. They said I could have a judge's hearing, but they kept trying to convince me that a road test would be quicker and simpler. I said no, because it was discriminatory. I continued to question them, and asked them if they had ever heard of the Americans with Disabilities Act (ADA).

I went home and began to research my rights. Online I reviewed the ADA sections that applied to my situation. I called the Medical Review board and was told all "challenged" individuals needed to take a road test and they had state laws that gave them that authority. I went to the Disability Center at school for advice and was told that this is what happens here in Arizona. The more I spoke with people, the more I realized that I needed to go forward with the hearing, not just for myself but for others as well. It became a matter of principle.

Three months later, in September 2002, a hearing was convened in the Executive Hearing Office of the Motor Vehicle Division, Arizona Department of Transportation in Flagstaff, Arizona. I went into the hearing capable of citing the Americans with Disabilities Act and knew that the Arizona Statutes quoted were invalid. Before the hearing commenced the judge looked at me and said, "You have caused a lot of havoc, young lady." I replied, "I am a woman of principle and this is wrong and discriminatory." In the end it was found that I was not required to complete a road test. Later I returned to the registry and a call was made to the Medical Review Board regarding what restrictions should be indicated on my license. Continued difficulties and ignorance arose when the woman at the Medical Review Board said to add hand controls to my license and list all of my adaptations in the vehicle. I got on the phone this time and told them that first of all, I have foot controls, not hand controls, and asked them why it was necessary to add a list of my adaptations. She stated that the list is needed if the vehicle has to be driven by someone other than myself. I firmly told her that no one drives my car except me and if they were to try, I would sue them. I hung up the phone and told the woman from the Registry my opinion about what restrictions she should put down. She agreed with me and I left.

After finally settling the matter of the license it was time to focus on the actual reason I had moved to Arizona. I was pursuing a master's degree in criminal justice. At the same time I needed to keep working while I got my education. Working and going to school was not easy. I worked about 25 hours a week at a runaway homeless shelter and then had a 10-hour graduate assistantship. I also had full-time classes and needed to write my thesis. On top of all that I did not know anyone in Flagstaff, Arizona. However, I was determined to succeed. I got myself on a schedule and made friends. One professor gave me some great advice. He said, "There is no way that you can do all the reading and writing for every single class, so you need to make choices". I learned that I could still do well in each class and get passing grades, even if I did not read every single assignment. I made sure that I went out with friends to de-stress. I also stayed focused, because as an out-of-state student I only had a two-year tuition waiver. This meant that if it took me more than two years to complete my degree I was going to have to pay out-of-state tuition. I was determined for that not to happen. That is who I am, and many people are amazed by this accomplishment. My close friend Julie has always been astonished by the way in which I wrote my thesis. A long time ago, back in physical therapy, I was taught how to type by using a pencil- poking method for each letter of the alphabet, and that is how I typed my entire masters thesis.

I had another ludicrous experience with the medical field while I was in Arizona. I went to the school clinic in order to refill a prescription. Before I could do that, they needed to check my blood pressure. They immediately asked how they could get a blood pressure reading on me. I explained to them that for most of my life my blood pressure had been taken down my upper leg. This became a problem immediately. First they did not know how to do it, and then they did not have the correct cuff. Despite my telling them that they needed a different cuff, they decided the cuff they had would work fine. My blood pressure ended up being high, and they were concerned, as was I. When I started to ask them questions the only answer they could give me was, "I do not know". They told me to come back in another couple of weeks and have my pressure checked again.

I got home that day and I called my dad, because I was worried. We had high blood pressure in the family. I remember asking him, "Does it make sense to have my blood pressure read the same on my leg as it would be on an arm"? "When you get your pressure done on your arm, does it matter how your arm is positioned"? My dad explained to me how important it was for your arm to be positioned in a particular way when you got your blood pressure taken. He agreed with me that my blood pressure should not be the same on my leg as it would be on somebody's arm.

When I brought this information back to the nurses again, they just did not know, and my blood pressure was still high, so they did not want to refill my prescription. By then, I was really annoyed. At this point the nurses wanted me to go on blood pressure medication because they had determined that I had high blood pressure. They felt it was necessary, yet still they could not answer any of my questions with anything other than, "I do not know". I was exasperated and demanded to see my doctor, who would be back on campus in just a couple of days. When I met with her she looked at me and said, "So you do not think you have high blood pressure". I said, "I do not think your nurses know what they are doing. Every time I ask a question the answer is, "I do not know", and now they want to put me on medication for high blood pressure. Again, all they say to me is, "I do not know." I am not going on medication without someone knowing something.

I related my conversation with my dad to her, and aired my concerns that my blood pressure should not be the same on my thigh as it would be on somebody's arm. She understood my feelings and found one of the nurses who had been there all summer. The Red Cross trained the nurse, so she and the doctor looked in the instruction manual to find out how to take an accurate blood pressure on somebody's thigh. After looking in the Red Cross book the doctor took my blood pressure accurately and realized that one's arms and one's thighs should not have the same blood pressure. She apologized for everything I had been put through during the summer and filled my prescription. This is a perfect example of how medical advocacy has been important in my life. Had I not spoken up they would have put me in high blood pressure pills when I did not have high blood pressure. Imagine what could have happened to my body.

The next time that I needed to advocate for myself with medical professionals was after moving home from Arizona. I had gone to a new primary care doctor and needed to get blood work done. They were not able to do the blood work at the clinic so they sent me to the hospital. Before going to the hospital I called in advance and explained my disability to them, and the fact that in order to take blood from me they had to take it from my foot. They assured me that this would not be a problem and we set up an appointment. When I got there nothing happened as planned. The staff proceeded to tell me that they were not allowed to take blood from my foot. They looked straight at me and told me they needed to take it from my arm. I said, "If you are not allowed to do it from my foot and I do not have any arms, what are you going to do?" They looked at me, very confused, and they decided that they should take it from my hand. Looking back I am not really sure why I agreed to this. It was very painful and totally unnecessary for them to take blood from my hand. After that experience I decided I was not going back to that doctor, nor was I going to get blood work done at that hospital ever again. The next time I got a new doctor I was far better at handling my self-advocacy. I explained the situation with my disability and described how to take blood for me. I made it very clear that they were going to do it the way that works for me, or not at all.

I am thankful for the laws in place today that have helped me fight against ignorance and the discriminatory actions of others. As a woman with a disability I have dealt with far too many ignorant people in my life. Most days I am an advocate, and I try to educate others about their ignorance, but there are those days when I am just too tired and do not want to deal with it. As a friend with a disability once said to me, there are some days when I just want to go to the grocery store, buy a gallon of milk, not talk to anybody, and go home.

Chapter 6
True Independence

We are...

We are capable of success

Just give us a little support

We are able do things that seem impossible

Just share some of your ideas with us

We are passionate and have strength despite all odds

Just hold some positive space for us

We are hard workers and contribute to society

Just allow us the opportunity

We are determined independent people

Just give us a chance

We are loving and capable parents

Just offer us tools to improve

We are intelligent and healthy individuals

Just spend time with us you will see

*L*earning skills allowed me to live an independent life. I started early and wove skills throughout the fabric of my days. It took me longer to learn to walk and dress myself, but it did happen. My family expected that I would achieve independence as other children do, but maybe with a little more time and patience. As a result, I believed the same thing. At times I would struggle with the need for more support, but in the end I succeeded.

For as long as I can remember, I have used a hook to dress myself. I started with a thick stick with a metal hook at one end. This was the "everyday" hook I used for dressing and sometimes for reaching. I had an alternate hook that was a long thin stick with a small hook at the end, which I used for zippers.

My parents understood how important it was for me to become independent, and they decided they would fabricate a tool that would help me with dressing, which had always been one of my greatest struggles. The everyday hook was created by taking a broom and cutting it down to about 21 inches. Then a metal hanger was formed into the shape of a hook and put into the end of the stick. That is my hook. Many of my doctors and therapists called it my "dressing stick". It was not easy to use my hook, nor did I always want to. Similar to many things in my life, nobody could actually teach me how to use it, because often their theoretical approaches did not match my reality. I needed to solve this problem on my own, and that took some time, as I struggled to figure out a way to use the hook to pull up my pants. It did not always work. The challenge was in finding just the right spot and pressure to make it useful. I finally learned that a combination of using my hand and my chin to make the hook work optimally.

As much as my hook provided me with independence, I also had to rely on it, and I didn't always feel good about that truth. I have a strong recollection of trying to put on my pajama pants without the hook. I was on the floor in the back bedroom of my grandparents' house. I determined that I could reach, or maybe I could wiggle, or somehow move in a way to get my pajama bottoms on without using the hook. I did get them on, but it took a lot of effort and I think that I pulled a muscle here and there. The important thing is that I succeeded. I was able to pull up the pajamas pants by being very flexible and wiggling. That success made me feel terrific, because I realized that there were times that I would be able to accomplish a task without the hook, and that mattered a great deal to me. With time, I realize that when I wear pants with an elastic waistband, I am able to pull off my pants by yanking one pant leg down with the other leg. Then I step on it a bit and pull a little more, and soon my pants are off. Mastering this skill made me feel less dependent on the hook.

The hook is a daily reminder of my difference, and when I was younger it was really hard on me. During school hours I kept the hook in my locker, which meant I always had to go back to my locker to retrieve it. This was uncomfortable and aggravating because I was often nowhere near my locker, and had to go across the school just to go to the restroom.

During my preteen years I really began to dislike my hook. There came a time when I went from hiding my hook at school to simply deciding that I did not need to go to the restroom until I got home. When the time came for sleepovers, I asked my parents to help construct something more subtle. The YWCA had sleepovers, but there was no way I could use the bathroom anywhere but home. I knew that I needed a travel hook because the existing hook did not fit in my backpack. At least that is what I told my parents, but there was more to the story: I needed a travel hook that could be hidden.

I remember the two trial hooks. The first one looked just like a ruler. It was flat and it folded up, which I thought would be perfect. Unfortunately, when I took it to a sleepover and tried to use it, it was not easy. Every time I put pressure on it to use it, it would start to fold. This was a big predicament. After much frustration I was forced to ask for help, which was awkward and embarrassing. I realized that it was critical that the new hook worked well before leaving my old hook at home. In this way I could avoid asking for help. The second hook was made of metal and had a spring in it. The idea was that you pushed down on it to make it longer and then pushed down to close it. This was great in theory, but in practice, not so good. When I went to use it I pushed down on it a bit too hard, and before I knew it the spring had sprung out of the metal and I jumped under the bed. Back to the drawing board my dad went, and the third attempt was perfect.

The hook I use today is an aluminum cylinder, which is collapsible into three sizes: 7, 14, or 21 inches. It fits in my purse easily, and is very light. When I first took my hook to school I had some difficulties. We had oiled it so it would open and close easily. Unfortunately, the oil caused it to keep sliding down, which made it too short. This made my trip to the restroom take much longer then usual, and the teacher came to check on me. This was embarrassing, but I soon figured out how to make this important tool work for me. Once I had the new hook I still continued to hide it when going to the restroom. It was small and black in color, and people hardly ever noticed it. As I got older I carried my hook with me all the time, which meant I needed to have a backpack or purse with me constantly.

I have grown to accept the hook as an extension of myself. I am no longer embarrassed by it, nor do I try to hide it when I have to use the restroom in a public place. There are times now that I walk out of a restroom without the hook collapsed, and I feel no awkwardness. It is something I have with me at all times, but I have learned that in an emergency a strong plastic hanger can be used. There have been a few times when I have left my hook in a different bag, and I've needed to figure out another option. Today I have three hooks, which is nice. I no longer need to switch my device in and out of bags so often, and have not needed the help of a hanger in a long time. The hook has given me an independence that would never have been possible. Now, when someone sees my tool I am open to questions, and see it as an opportunity to educate another person about disability. I have even shared my hook with other people with TARs, and it has helped them to become more independent.

Having a hook gave me autonomy with regard to personal care, but there were still independent living skills that I had yet to learn. Washing my own hair was a big one. My mom was there to help me when I needed it, and I never had a problem asking for that help. I think many of us learn new things out of need. One night I had finished my bath and was waiting for my mom to come and wash my hair. I remember yelling to let her to let know I was ready. She said she would be coming right along. I was growing impatient, and minutes felt like hours. I started wondering why I couldn't just wash my own hair. I knew I needed to be able to reach my head with shampoo. The solution was easy: use my foot. First I grabbed the shampoo and put some on the bottom of my foot. Then I brought my head and foot together and scrubbed. I had been able to wrap my legs around my neck for years, so this was easy. Working out the task of rinsing took a little more thought. My mom usually ran the water and used a cup, which was clearly not going to work when I did it myself. Instead, I just ran the water and lay down underneath it. This technique worked well for almost all the rinsing, but reaching the hair closest to my head was a little more difficult. Then I remembered how my sisters flipped their heads upside down to blow-dry their hair. I sat up, crossed my legs, flipped my head forward and put it under the water, and it worked. My hair was clean! The next challenge was getting out of the tub.

Exiting the tub was a little daunting, as I had never done it on my own. At the time my legs were not as strong as they are today, and balancing on one leg was really difficult. There was also the problem of the slippery tub. At this point, finishing this undertaking before Mom arrived had become a matter of principle. I slowly stood up, holding onto the wall as best as I could; then I brought one leg over the side of the bathtub. I remember my leg shaking, and worrying that I might fall. Once I got the first leg over I was all set because there was a dry mat to steady me on the ground, and before I knew it I was out. As I sit here writing, I wonder why I never thought to sit on the side of the tub and bring my legs around instead of stepping out, since it would have been much easier. Hindsight makes it simple to look back on a situation and find uncomplicated solutions. The reality is that Mom always held my hand as I got out, and so getting out while standing was what I was used to doing. I quickly grabbed a towel and ran downstairs to tell my mom what I had accomplished.

My mother and sisters always helped with my hair. I was able to brush my hair easily, and now I could wash it myself as well. Having long hair, I often wanted to wear a ponytail, and making one was something I did not know how to do on my own. One day I got a brush and an elastic band and found a big open place on the ground. I gave my hair a good brushing and then put the elastic between my toes and brought my feet to my head. The first problem was the angle, and that was impossible to change because my ankles do not move the way wrists move. The next issue was trying to hold my hair and an elastic between my toes and then wrap the elastic around the hair. It was not happening, despite my best efforts. Before I stopped trying, my Mom came upstairs and was bewildered by what I was trying to do. When I told her, she shook her head and walked away. She knew that when I got something in my head I needed either to puzzle it out to a solution, or decide it was not essential. After a while I realized that I was not going to be successful, despite how hard I tried. Today, when people ask me what I cannot do, I tell them I can't put my hair in a ponytail. They often seem puzzled by my answer. A few years ago I met a woman without arms or hands, and she often wore a ponytail. I thought she must have known how to make it work! When I asked her how she did it , she said, "I have other people do it". So the method I use to put my hair in a ponytail without having arms is… asking for help.

I have written quite a bit about hair, but what about other important aspects of being a young girl? As a person who has a disability I have not always been able to wear the same clothes as my friends. When I was younger, sometimes it bothered me. As I got older the clothing situation definitely had an impact on my life. Footwear has been one of my largest topics of concern, both as a child and still as an adult. At first, I wore plastic & metal leg braces that started at the top of my thigh and went all the way down to the bottom my foot. If you have ever seen the movie Forrest Gump, I had braces that were similar to his, but they stopped at the top of my thigh. Finding a pair of jeans that fit easily over my braces was extremely difficult. Buying a pair of shoes that I could put on myself over these braces was even more difficult. I spent most of my childhood in Velcro sneakers, because if I had laced sneakers I could not reach to tie them. There were times when I did not have to wear my braces and I was able to wear shoes that had no Velcro. As these opportunities arose, my physical therapist and my parents realized that I needed to learn to tie my shoes. Here is my technique:

We started with an 8 x 11 piece of stiff paper, with a picture of a shoe that had holes in it to allow you to "lace" the shoe. The lacing part was pretty easy and I was able to do it one-handed, which was essential, as my hands cannot reach other. But then there was the tying. My physical therapist encouraged me to use one hand and hold it against the paper in order to loop the laces through. I tried it several times. After struggling and being a bit frustrated with the whole process, I decided just to do what felt natural. I used my mouth and lips. I put the laces between my lips, which allowed me to anchor them in place, make a loop, and pull it through. Once I had accomplished shoe tying on the picture, I tried it while my shoes were on my feet. As with most things in life, one foot was easier than the other. My right foot is not as flexible, and so working with it was more difficult than my left, especially since when I tied my left shoe I could use my right hand, which is dominant. I found I just needed to wiggle a little more and take a little more time, and then my shoes would be tied. I also learned to tie other people's shoes with my toes. This was extremely useful as I got older and started babysitting.

In junior high school my options for clothing underwent a big change. I got new braces that were smaller and more stylish. My doctor also told me that I did not need to wear the braces every day anymore. This meant I could look into wearing different clothing, but that also meant I needed to figure out how to make that clothing accessible. I was 15 before I owned a pair of jeans that I could put on and take off entirely by myself. There are a couple of problems with jeans for me: the snap or button and the zipper. As a freshman in high school I came across a pair of hip-hugger jeans. There was no snap or button to deal with and the zipper had a really big opening that my hook fit through perfectly. I could slide the hook into the opening of the zipper and pull it up or down easily. After I wore these jeans somebody in the family came up with the idea of taking a small keychain and attaching it to the zipper of standard jeans or pants. At last I was able to pull the zipper up and down. This was exciting because it was possible for me to buy pants without an elastic waist. My final issue was with the button, but then my sister came up with the idea of not using the button at all. She explained that the jeans were not going to fall down because I have hips. I kept my pants unbuttoned for a while, but then tried adding Velcro. Between the Velcro and a small keychain, I have been able to wear any pants I choose.

Shopping for clothes is one the activities I dislike most. When I go shopping, I am on a mission. I look for the item that I need, and if I find it, great. If I do not, I am out of there. I have never been one to scan the racks up and down for hours. I discovered early on that when I do that my legs begin to hurt very quickly. Then I am stuck in a store where there are no chairs, with legs that hurt, and if I sit on the floor I am told to get up because it is dirty. I have never really listened to the directive to get off the floor, because I have always figured I would wash the clothes later anyway.

As an adult I realize that it is not socially acceptable to sit on the floor in a store, but still do it if I need too.

The other problem with shopping for clothes is that nothing fits me properly, and since I need to wear short sleeves year-round it becomes difficult to find warm clothing for the winter. When I was a child I also had to deal with leg braces, and I can tell you that finding pants that can be worn over braces is a nightmare. You can see why shopping has never been fun for me. Many of the same issues I had as a child exist for me still, so I am not much of a shopper even today. When I buy a pair of pants, if they are not elastic on top I need to have a button or zipper changed to Velcro, and then I must shorten the pants as well. This is an added cost to an already expensive pair of pants. On top of needing to get the pants fixed before I can wear them for work. I also need to bring someone shopping with me because I cannot button or zip the pants in the dressing room. The process of buying and finally being able to wear a pair of dress pants is exhausting.

I do not even pretend to shop for shirts unless it is warm out. Luckily, there are various short-sleeved shirts around in the summer. I have also found that over the last 10 years short-sleeved sweaters have been in fashion. I am still not sure why somebody with arms would want to own short-sleeved sweaters and wear them in the winter, but I am grateful for that because now I have some lovely, fashionable sweaters. I also have found that some stores that cater to professional women carry short-sleeved tops year-round because they anticipate wearing them under a jacket. There are, of course, other obstacles that clothing presents for me, including zippers on skirts and dresses that I cannot manage. I suspect that I will never own a suit because I am not sure how I would be able to button the suit jacket.

Undergarments are a whole different kind of fun for me. Many people do not realize that my shoulders are not positioned in a similar fashion to most women and therefore, straps fall down. Bra straps often fell down on me until I discovered that I could buy racer back bras. I need to make sure there is a stretch to them, because I cannot do the snaps after I put them on. My hook has allowed me to dress myself, but it has put more holes in my underwear than one can imagine. I wore tights under my braces when I was a child, and hated them. In the first place I had to wear them all the time and they were never comfortable. Also, they were really difficult to put on, using a hook. I went through many pairs of tights because I would put holes in them with the hook. As an adult I refuse to wear them. There was a time that I wore pantyhose. I did an okay job of not putting holes in the pantyhose with the hook, but that was a horrendous effort, and I decided that that was a battle that I did not need in my life.

Now we must talk a little more about shoes, since they are nightmarish as well. I once had a physical therapist ask me if he could take a picture of my feet to use in his class. Apparently my feet are examples of much of the subject matter he was teaching his students. I have flat feet; I walk pigeon-toed and heavy on the inside of my feet; I have a high instep; my feet are wide; I have five toes, however my fourth toe sits on top of my fifth. Let's not forget that as an adult I wear a child's size 2 shoe. When I was in college I went shoe shopping with my friend Jackie. After the sixth shoe store she vowed never to go shoe shopping with me again.

Being a woman with a disability has presented me with some interesting challenges. When I was a child I did not have that much interest in the "girly" part of life. The mere thought of owning a dress or skirt was horrible to me. As I got older those feelings began to change. Shaving my legs was something that I needed to learn how to do. I grew up in a household with three other women and therefore, had access to a razor. I started shaving when I was about 12 years old, mainly because the hair on my legs bothered me. It was not vanity; it is just that I use my legs and feet for everything. As I got older my legs would brush up against each other and I could feel the hair on my skin, which I didn't like. When I was younger I shaved from the knee down, and that was pretty easy. I put the razor between my toes and then I shaved. When I got older my father was able to make an attachment to my hook that allowed the razor to fasten. I used this attachment to shave other areas that were harder to reach, through college. Then one day, a friend suggested waxing. At first I was not comfortable with the idea, but as I got older and grew more confident about my body, I realized waxing was so much easier for me.

When I began high school, I started to care more about my appearance. I started to take care of my own hair, makeup and nail polish. Accomplishing all of these tasks took a bit of practice. When I was in high school "big hair" was the thing. You can believe that was actually pretty hard to achieve, one handed. There was a complicated process I went through to do it myself. First, I sat down on the toilet and turned my hair upside down. Then I sprayed the hair to hold it in place, and flipped my head back up. The biggest challenge the hairspray presented was trying to spray it upside down. Time was never on my side. I found that I only had a few seconds before I needed to stop, to angle my head so that it was not exactly upside down. Once the hair was done, there was makeup to apply.

Makeup was something that I did not know much about, but I still attempted it. I used both my hands and my feet when putting on makeup. I still do, to this day. Usually I sit on the floor and hold a mirror between my toes. Then I use one of my hands to put on makeup, whether it is blush or eye shadow. Applying eye shadow has never been fun because I cannot reach to hold one eyelid down and look in the mirror with the other, so I just have to put it on slowly and hope for the best. I have been comfortable with a powder cover-up, as that is not as tricky to manage. Blush and lipstick have always been pretty easy for me to apply.

Learning to polish my nails well was tough. At first, I tried hard to bring my hands together and put the nail polish on. As time went on I realized that that was not the best way to accomplish this undertaking, because it took a really long time and it was a bit painful. I decided to do this the way I did most things: the easiest way possible. Now I open the bottle of nail polish with my teeth. I hold the nail polish brush between my lips and I rest my hands either on my foot or on another high surface. Then I paint my nails. Painting my toenails is a little different. I usually use my hands more. My left foot is always easy to do because it is very flexible and I can reach it as I do when tying my shoes. My right foot I have to twist a little bit more, and it is not as easy for me to get the nails done. When I was in high school I got really good at polishing my nails. I could even do a French manicure on myself. I was a cashier at a movie theater and I would get many compliments on my nails. That was especially flattering since I painted them myself!

I don't usually give much thought to all the things that I do in my everyday life. My theory is that I need to find a way to do the job, and once I find it, that is excellent. As I have gotten older I realize that my life can be interesting to other people. Take polishing my nails, for example. I have been able to paint my nails without help since I was a kid. This is not a big deal to me. About a year ago I was at a friend's house. There were a bunch of us, just hanging out. At some point during the day one of the women got nail polish out and was painting her nails. I saw that she was using the same color nail polish that I had on my nails, and I knew that my nails were chipped. I asked her if it would be okay to use some of her polish to fix my nails. She had no problem with it and I was excited. I did ask her to open the nail polish for me. Although I would normally use my teeth to do that, I did not want to use my teeth on somebody else's nail polish and possible leave marks. I proceeded to hold the nail polish as I normally would, between my toes, and use my lips to paint my nails. The next thing I knew, the room was completely quiet. I looked up to see what was so interesting and found everybody studying me with astonishment. They were all mesmerized, watching me paint my nails, and pretty much in awe that I could do it so well by holding the brush in a most unconventional way.

At a certain point in my youth, my mother told me that if I didn't start putting the laundry away I would be washing it myself. Sure enough, I did not put it away and she told me I had to do my own laundry. The first time that I did laundry it was not easy. I believe my Mom turned the water on for me and helped me open the lid on the machine, and then I loaded the clothes. Getting the clothing out of the washer was the most difficult thing for me. My first plan was to use my hook, because I thought it would give me enough reach to get to the bottom of the washer. Although it did give me the distance, the clothes were wet and heavy. The process was really slow and I think I even pulled a muscle in my neck by the end of it. Taking things out of the dryer was not too bad. I just opened the door and pretty much leaned my whole body into the dryer to pull closer.

The next time I did laundry I figured out that it was easier to climb up on top of the dryer and sit there. The dryer was next to the washer, and I could bring my feet over and reach into the washer to pull the clothes out, and then throw them into the dryer. This was a much quicker process and I did not pull any muscles. I did manage not to have to do laundry for a while, though, because when my mom realized that she needed to clear off the top of the dryer permanently in order for me to sit on it to do laundry, she decided she would rather do my laundry than keep the dryer clear. A win for me!

Doing laundry became quite a chore again when I went to college. My father put the laundry bin on wheels for me so it would be easy for me to get it down to the campus laundry. Then I would climb up on top of things much as I had when I was at home. I did try to bring my clothes home as often as possible, because it was much easier. When I moved off campus to my own apartment, washing clothes was difficult yet again. I used the same laundry basket my dad had made for me. My friends and I would go down to the Laundromat a couple of blocks away from the house. None of us had a car, so we pushed our bins down the street. The Laundromat was not handicapped accessible, so my friends helped me get my clothes out of the washer into the dryer, as the washers and dryers were not next to one another.

When I moved to Arizona I had a telephone conversation with my sister, Christine that forever changed how I do laundry. Apparently when she lived in the city she brought her clothing to the Laundromat and paid somebody else to do it. I thought she was crazy and knew it would be expensive. I didn't really know anybody in Arizona, and the first few times I went to the Laundromat on my own, I had to ask total strangers to help me. I decided that Christine might be on to something, so I checked with the Laundromat and sure enough, you could drop off your laundry and they would wash and dry and fold it and you could pick it up later. So that is how I did laundry while in graduate school and until I got my own washer and dryer in my apartment.

The kitchen has never been easy for me. I am 4" 11' and I have no arms, and so I cannot reach at least 50% of the kitchen. If the microwave is on a counter, I am happy. If it is placed over the stove, it presents a problem. I can sometimes turn on stovetops if the knobs are in front, but not so much if they are in the back. People asked me what I do about cooking. I tell them that I cook only because I need food to survive. There have been many challenges for me regarding cooking. Let's start with boiling water. This should be easy. You just put water in the pot, bring it to the burner, and turn the burner on. For me, however, this could be very difficult, depending upon how my kitchen was set up. To fill a pot of water I need a step stool, and then I have to gain access to the faucet. Turning on the faucet usually means using my chin or head. Then I need to get the pot of water from the sink to the stove. When a counter connected my stove and sink, this was usually a pretty easy task, as I was able just to slide the pot gently over to the burner. Turning the burners on has been easier in some houses than others. If the knobs are in the front it is rather easy. When they have been in the back I have needed to find inventive ways to get to them.

Nowadays I do not have a counter that connects my sink and stove. That means that I must fill up the pot of water and slowly walk over to the stove, to the burner. I need to be careful about not having the water too high, which would make the pot too heavy to carry. I also have to be even more careful when I need to drain the water after boiling, so that I won't burn myself. Making a task easier is really just a matter of perspective. People are often curious as to how I use the oven. An oven is an appliance that I stay far away from, because other than opening it when it is not turned on, it is just not safe to work one without arms. So the answer to how I use the oven is easy: I do not. When I was a child my parents always had a small toaster oven, and I used that growing up. Ultimately I realized that you could cook just about anything in a toaster oven. You can imagine my excitement when I found a toaster oven that opens from right to left and not top to bottom. This little machine does everything… toasts, broils, bakes, and roasts. It even has a rotisserie. It is true that it is difficult to make food for more than two people in a toaster oven, but at this point in my life, it is working perfectly for me.

How about the simple task of putting the cover on a pot? I managed to complete both college and graduate school without ever covering a pot. If I were to put the top on a pot, once the food was ready I wouldn't be able to get the top off without burning myself. That situation changed one day after I moved back from Arizona and spent four months living with my parents. My father walked into the kitchen one day, looked at me and saw the water set to boil. He asked why I didn't put the cover on the pot, so it would boil faster. I looked at him and said, "I can't." I asked him if I put the cover on the pot, once the food was ready, how was I supposed to get it off? He answered, "Yes, I can see that being a problem". You might think that this was the end of the discussion, but you probably have the idea by now that my father didn't like to hear me say, "I can't" about anything.

The next day my dad came to the kitchen with a little wooden tool. He looked at me and said, "Sheila, come over here and see if this works for you". He created an implement that gave me the extension of an arm and could also grasp a cover. This tool allowed me to lift the cover off boiling water without burning myself. It worked perfectly the first time. Dad went on to add a magnet to it so it could hang on the side of the refrigerator. The original tool was crafted specifically for the pots in my family's kitchen, but when I moved he made one for my own pots and pans.

My parents did their best to make the kitchen accessible for me growing up. My cups and plates were in a cabinet close to the ground. We had the microwave on the counter, and the food that I was likely to eat was kept on the lower shelves. When I wanted items that were out of my reach, I did what every other kid would do… I climbed. I used a chair to get onto the counter. Then I stood on the counter opening cabinets to get my snack. I was lucky that my parents never saw me do this because I think it might have made them a little crazy.

The refrigerator has always been a challenge. I have two options when getting things out of the fridge: I can dive into it and try not to hit my head, or I can use my feet. I have found myself doing a little bit of both. If there are items in the front, I just reach in and do my best to avoid hitting my head. With items in the back of the refrigerator, I stand on one leg and move things around with my other leg. Then I pull them up to the front and grab them with my hand. I can stand on a step stool to reach into the freezer. Sometimes I stand on one leg to reach, or I use my hook. Many people find the methods I have developed to navigate life pretty interesting. To me it is just the reality of my everyday life.

During my college years, I have a distinct memory of being at a friend's apartment. I wanted a glass of milk, so I went into the kitchen to get one. The milk was on the top shelf of the fridge, in the back. Without giving it much thought, I took off my sock and stood on one leg and proceeded to move things around in the fridge. I guess I was feeling a little lazy that day, so instead of grabbing the milk with my hand once it was up front, I grabbed it with my toes and laid it carefully on the floor. I heard a small gasp, and turned to see my friend standing in the doorway. She was completely amazed by what she had just seen, I shrugged my shoulders. No big deal for me.

Another not-so-fun kitchen activity is washing dishes. Growing up with a dishwasher, I never had to worry much about it. If I needed to clean dishes they went in the dishwasher. When I was about nine my family went camping and my friend and I decided to help my mom with the dishes. Water overflowed the sink, dripping down the cabinets onto the floor. When my mom came back she suggested that it might be best if we did not wash the dishes again without her. I took her suggestion seriously and I did not wash a dish again until I was in college.

At 19 I was in college and living on campus. Living independently my first year was pretty easy. There were some minor accommodations made, and I used a stepladder when I needed it. The summer arrangements were a little different.

The summer after my freshman year I lived in an apartment with a few of my friends. I truly do not know why I gave no thought to accessibility until after I moved in. There were definitely some problems. The kitchen sink was very deep and I could not reach the bottom of it. I stood in front of our huge, deep sink, which was attached to the wall without any counter space around it. I had no clue how I was going to wash dishes. I could not use my feet, as there was no counter space to sit on. As it was, I even had concerns about putting dishes in the sink. I was afraid I would break them because it was so deep. My roommates were helpful, and one even thought of the idea of a sponge on a stick. The stick was hollow and filled with dish detergent. When you flipped it, the detergent would seep into the sponge and you could wash dishes. It's the same tool that I use to this day, and when I am feeling kind of lazy I jump up on the counter and wash the dishes with my feet.

The apartment was on the second floor with steep stairs. But; the idea of living on my own with my friends was so exciting I was willing to meet any challenge. I learned to function well there, and as with anything else, each challenge met made me stronger.

My sophomore year I lived on campus in a school apartment, which was more accessible than my summer one, but still presented difficulties. At the end of the year my parents gave me the choice either to move home and commute or find an apartment off campus with friends. It was an easy choice.

I ended up moving back in with the same friends I had lived with the previous summer. They lived in Worcester and I went to school in Boston, so I had a significant commute. This apartment was definitely more accessible than the summer apartment, but there were still issues. Cooking on the stove was difficult because the knobs were in the very back. I made it work by using one of my hooks, but it was not easy. I had problems with the front door knob, too. I was locked in my apartment at least three times because I was not physically capable of turning the knob and opening the door. It took a bit of persuasion, but we did manage to get our landlord to replace the doorknob with a latch that made it possible for me to open and close the door easily.

It was not until I moved to Arizona that I really began to realize that I needed to think more about accessibility in my living quarters. I had moved 3,000 miles away from home and I was on my own. My apartment in graduate school was extremely accessible. It was on the ground floor, the countertops and even the cabinets were pretty low. The most significant accommodation I needed was with the mailbox, which needed to be lower. The landlords provided me with that and went on to give me a reserved parking spot that was close to my apartment.

In my current life, looking for an apartment presents multiple challenges. It needs be on either the ground level floor or provide an elevator. I need more kitchen space than most people, since cabinets need to be on the floor. It is helpful for me to simply jump up on the sink to wash dishes. I need off-street parking, especially living on the East Coast with all the snow that we get here. And finally, I need to make sure that I have a bathtub. There have been many times I have gone without one because I figured I could make do, but I have reached a time in my life when I need a few things that work well for me.

Today I live completely independently. When I was a child, people said I would never be independent. It's true that there are things that I cannot do on my own: changing the shower curtain, for one, or changing a light bulb, for another. I understand that even when I ask my able-bodied friends, there are certain things they cannot do. I am so grateful to live an independent life, but when I need them, my amazing friends and family are always there to lend me a hand.

Chapter 7
The Giver

My World

I navigate my world unlike you....
And yet you watch me with intent.
For years I have been baffled by this.
Why are you interested in my world?

I see the world as a puzzle.
Each task I work out in my mind before.
I watch you to see how I should do it differently.
A two step task for you; is six or eight for me

Is your watch of judgment or of wonder?
Your eyes portray a mixture of both.
Why does my world hold your interest?

Is the judgment due to fear or ignorance?
You hold no understanding, and yet you want to…
And so you assume the truth.

You hold silent when you could speak your questions.
That silence sees my world as difficult and unpleasant
When it is simple and beautiful

The wonder you hold keeps my curiosity.
Your excitement grows as you watch my steps
Silence fills the room; did I miss something?
No, you are merely watching me

Your mind is full of questions, and they are wonderful.
My answers give truth to the puzzle of my life.
No longer must you wonder how; for I am here to show and tell.

I saw myself in my own world
And I watched with wonder.
How interesting I found each task.

The puzzle in my mind; I now can see.
I watch with intent, what happens next
How interesting it is, I have watched you for years but not myself.

I navigate my world unlike you.
You watch me with intent.
Now I understand this.

My world is different, full of surprise and adventure.
Why wouldn't you want to come and see!

*P*aying it forward has always been important to me. I think I understood from a young age that I was lucky to have received so much from others. I knew, as I grew older, aware of how much I have received, that I wanted to become a giver. When I turned 21, my services from Shriners' Hospital for Children ended, but before I left I asked one thing of them: Please call me if there was anything that I could do for them, if there was anyone I could help. Since that day Shriners' has taken me up on my offer a few times.

In my mid-twenties I was asked to speak to Shriners' donors, so they could truly understand how Shriners' makes a difference in people's lives. Speaking just before me was a physical therapist who explained different adaptive tools children were using at the hospital. When it was my turn to speak I began by saying that although we just heard valuable information about adaptive tools, I do not use any of them. The crowd roared with laughter, which gave me a nice transition into my story and an explanation of everything that Shriners' had done for me. I also told them about the adaptations that I used in my life that made it easier for me to live independently.

Shriners' contacted me to help a new patient. They explained that there was a young man from Poland who had lost both of his arms in an accident. They were hoping that my coming to speak to him would help him see that his life could be still very fulfilling. It was a great experience meeting him, and we had some fine conversations about how I did things with my legs and feet. It definitely was going to be different for him because he had not spent his life using his lower body the way I had, but I think I was able to inspire him and help him through a difficult time. Shriners offered me the opportunity to mentor people with all kinds of disabilities, and gave me a chance to educate others. As I grew older my world expanded, and I soon learned that there other people in the world who were like me... some older, some younger. I became the mentor I had always longed for in my own life

Can you imagine living the first 23 years of your life without the memory of ever meeting another person who looked like you or really understood you? Can you imagine living in a world where society expected you to fail? Can you imagine that every time you accomplished a task, it was a way of proving yourself to the world?

Becoming a mentor to other children with Tar Syndrome has been very important to me. My parents told me that when I was a baby they met an 18-year-old young man with Tar Syndrome. This meeting gave my parents hope that someday I would be independent, noting that he was able to do many things on his own. They have also told me that they knew of two other children born with Tar Syndrome, one six months older than I and one six months younger. Unfortunately, both of them moved far away, and I have no memory of ever meeting either of them. The only memory that I have of another person with Tar Syndrome is a conversation I had on the phone when I was a teenager. It was with the same young man that my parents had met when I was a baby. All I remember of that conversation was that he drove a car and flew a plane with his feet.

The first face-to-face meeting I had with another person with Tar Syndrome occurred when I was in college. That meeting taught me that there were different types of Tar Syndrome, which I never knew. I learned that I have short-armed TARs and the woman I met had long-armed TARs. I also came away from that experience realizing that the only thing I had in common with the other woman was our disability, and unfortunately, that was not be enough to sustain a friendship.

It would be another five years before I had the opportunity to mentor a child with TAR Syndrome. Shriners' called me regarding Michael, a two-year-old boy with Tar Syndrome. His parents hoped to meet someone else who had TARs, to give them guidance about how best to support their son.

This was a great opportunity, since as it was only the second time I met someone with Tar Syndrome. We agreed to exchange phone numbers and before I knew it I received a call from Misty, Michael's mother. Five years later we are still good friends. I have been supportive of the family as they make decisions about their son. This relationship has repeatedly reminded me of everything my parents did for me.

Michael was about 2 1/2 years old when we met. My first telephone conversation with Misty lasted at least two hours. She asked me innumerable questions about my childhood. She wanted to know how my parents figured out what to do for me and what she should do for Michael. I remember very well when we finally met. It was a cold winter day and the whole family came rushing into my apartment. Michael's was carried in and placed on the floor. His parents went back to get things out of the car, and so Michael and I had a moment alone. I sat down next to him, and for a moment my whole life flashed in front of my eyes. I was full of tears, both for Michael and myself, remembering all the pain and anguish I went endured as a child. As quickly as the tears came, they disappeared, and I noticed the sparkle in his eyes. I could see that this young guy was a fighter and I knew he had a family that supported him. I could tell that he was going to be able to figure things out.

The rest of the afternoon, we just hung out. We played some games and we talked. It was a nice time. Misty and I have spoken on the phone hundreds of times since that day. I have done my best to be a friend and advocate. I went to Shriners' Hospital for Children with Misty, Johnny and Michael. They already had an appointment, but I insisted we should meet with Dr. Drvaric, the head of surgery. Amazingly, within a short period time, the chief surgeon arrived. He brought my medical records along with Michael's. He spoke with all of us about how Michael's form of Tar Syndrome was different from mine. There were different options for him. In the end, Michael was not a patient at Shriners'. I was happy when Michael found the right doctor. Since then Michael has had major surgery, which has enabled him to walk. Although his path has been different from mine, I have been there to support him and his family going forward to this day.

They say the Internet has made the world smaller, and I definitely agree with that. Because of Facebook, I now know about 100 people with Tar Syndrome, from all over the world. Through Facebook, I met a 16-year-old girl with TARS who lives in New Jersey. We chatted online for a while and I gave her tips about dressing and other daily activities. It has been great getting to know her and I even had the opportunity to meet her when her brother was moving to Boston for college. It is exciting to be able to explain to her how I do things like wash my hair, drive my car and live without assistance. Our friendship has really made an impact on her life. On her senior year trip in high school, she was able to go without having another person there to help her with her daily activities.

I have ongoing relationships with people who have Tar Syndrome on Facebook. The groups have allowed me to share my life experiences, make friendships, and inspire others with what I've accomplished. I look forward to the opportunity to meet more people with Tar Syndrome, develop friendships, and help them through their life struggles as best I can.

Reflecting on my life thus far, I have had successes and failures, encouragement and discrimination, compromises, hospitalizations, family life, school, a professional career and ultimately self-acceptance. Through determination, loving support and resilience, I have built a life of independence. Today I am a self-sufficient woman who has beaten the odds.

Motivational speaking has created an avenue for me to share my story with the world. It's important for people to believe in themselves, and if they really want to achieve something it will be possible... it just might take some time. We all have hard times, and we all need time to cry. But just when you think you can't go on, you get up and start over again. Each of us has the power to live our lives as we want to live them; we just need to accept the challenges around us and move forward. Others can learn from me that you never have to give up. I have undertaken so much in my life. I have an indomitable spirit, and sometimes I wanted to do what looked impossible, and sometimes I just wanted to prove to the world that I could do it. My family will tell you that the best way to help me to succeed is to tell me I cannot do something. Even when things fall apart, I find the light.

I often contemplate the idea of inspiring others. I have been through so much in my life, and when people know my story it is inspirational. But sometimes - random strangers approach me I can be walking down the street, or in the grocery store, or sitting at a table. People will come up to me and say, "Wow! You're such an inspiration.". It can be frustrating. I am simply living my life. It is just a life like anyone else's. Oddly, it also feels like a slap in the face sometimes, because I do not want to be inspiration simply by walking down the street. I succeed in life because of my friends, family and the community around me. I have learned to be myself and to believe in myself. It's okay to have tough days; tomorrow might bring sunshine. The difficult times in life are not always the bad times. Our greatest challenges are our greatest teachers, and we learn from the thorniest times in our lives.

My family has always been there to protect me and be present for me. My mom created a motto that I have lived by all my life: "The impossible only takes a little longer." My dad always reminded me that the most important four letters of "American" are "I can". My parents raised me with a positive attitude that has helped me to live in an able- bodied society. I have always been treated as an equal member of the family. Having a disability was never an excuse not to do something. Often we needed to figure out how I might complete a task, but that was all. It was never a question of if. It was always a question of how.

Chapter 8
Driving Forward

Voice

My inner voice has broken free....
Once limited,
Once timid,
Once silent.

My inner voice speaks aloud and questions,
Why must I follow you?
Why should I be silent?
Why can there be no change?

My inner voice denies your power and speaks of change.
Rules are meant to be broken.
Yesterday's truths are today's lies.
Change starts with a single notion.

My voice has joined with others.
Together, the world is different.
Together, other paths are visible.
Together, notions of change are growing.

Voice is now
Massive
Strong
Loud

Voice teaches
Strength
Possibilities
Acceptance

Voice is an agent of change.

My voice has brought me full-circle
Once hidden,
Now it represents the masses.

*F*rom the time I was a young girl, driving was on the top of my list of things to accomplish. Unlike my friends, learning to drive was a major challenge for me. People humored me, nodding and smiling when I told them I was going to drive with my feet one day.

I got my learner's permit twice during high school. I went to the DMV with my friends, showed my passport, paid the fee, and took the exam. Before I knew it I had my permit. Driving was unsafe for me, so I did not use my permit often. I drove exactly three times when I had my permit, each time in parking lots. I used my hands and drove slowly, realizing each time how essential it was for me to have adaptions to my vehicle. When I was younger, I got to drive a golf cart and a boat.

One weekend I was camping with my family, and at some point we got into a conversation about golf carts and how I wanted to learn to drive one. Maureen, one of the owners of the campground, was all for it. The next thing I knew we were in the back part of the campground, ready to get going on the golf cart. Maureen gave me a few instructions, and soon we were driving. It was easy until I got up to speed. The high position of the steering wheel was great for me, because there was no bending or pain.

The ride was going smoothly until I needed to make a fast turn. I bumped into a picnic table. I didn't think I hit it that hard, but it fell apart. In my defense, the picnic table looked ready to fall apart. Overall, it was a really enjoyable afternoon, and we had the bonus of a lot of wood for the campfire that evening.

My next driving experience was in high school. My friend Jamie's dad had a boat and we were out on the water when he asked us if we wanted to drive. It was great fun! I remember it being one of the easiest vehicles that I had ever tried to drive. I did not have to worry so much about the gas and brake at same time. Jamie's father stood behind me so we knew that we would be safe. I only needed to use one hand, which made it even simpler for me, and before we knew it we were driving all around the lake. I did really well and there was no crashing this time!

I knew that driving would be difficult for me, but I was determined. When I was sixteen, I learned that Mass Rehab could help me once I turned twenty-one, I did not mind the wait, since I was looking into college in the city and did not need a car right away. When I turned twenty-one, I called the Boston office of Mass Rehab and arranged my orientation. I was disappointed to learn that it would be a two-year wait until I could receive the funding necessary for a modified vehicle.

Just before graduation, the Massachusetts Rehabilitation Vehicle Modification Program contacted me. After a two-year wait they were ready to adapt a vehicle for me. The Mass Rehab representative said that I should shop for a vehicle immediately but hold off on buying it until they gave their go-ahead. I was told that a driver's assessment was required, to evaluate my driving needs and physical abilities.

The entire process was quite a learning experience. My driving evaluation was scheduled at a rehabilitation center in New Hampshire. The assessment covered a number of things. There were discussions about my medical history, my fine motor skills, cognitive skills, reaction time, and strength proficiencies. Then I was asked if I preferred to steer with my hands or my feet. I quickly replied, "Feet", because I could not imagine steering a vehicle with my hands.

The next step of the assessment was to review adaptive devices. I was shown a van with various controls. I was able to try toggle switches, push pads, head switches, hand controls, joysticks, and foot controls. The assessor then documented which adaptive devices would fit my needs. After Mass Rehab received my assessment I was instructed to purchase an American- made vehicle because I required foot steering. Additionally, I needed to make sure that there was eight to ten inches of space between the brake pedal and the left side of the car. The car could not be more then three years old, with an odometer reading less than fifty thousand miles.

I educated myself about buying a car. When I was ready, my friends and family helped me with my search. My experiences at dealerships were extremely frustrating. I went with a list of specific requirements, and several times the sales representatives disregarded my requests and showed me cars that did not meet my needs. At other times the salesperson would speak to whomever I had with me, after I had clearly told them I was the one buying the car. This behavior angered me and I felt they were discriminating against me because of my disability. I walked out of several dealerships. I had experienced enough discrimination in my life and I was determined to enjoy buying my first car.

I called insurance companies to find out how to get my car insured once it was purchased. In the year 2000 Massachusetts was a noncompetitive state for insurance, and the rates were extremely high. I was in tears as I called insurance company after insurance company. I just did not know how I would afford a car loan and car insurance on my income. Getting a second job was out of the question, as I was already in school full time with a part-time job. I was also commuting on public transportation, which doubled my travel time. In addition, finding a different job was difficult, as my physical disability limited my choices. However, there was hope! One insurance company asked me how long I had been driving. I responded that I did not have a license and this would be my first car. I also mentioned that I would need modifications on my vehicle. The agent was extremely helpful, and suggested that I contact a family member with a good driving record and have that person insure my car. This was a great relief. My dad agreed to insure my car under his name, and the fee became manageable. It is people like this insurance agent that have helped make so many things possible for me.

In early December of 2000, I bought a 1999 Oldsmobile Intrigue. My dad insured the car, but I was the owner. I did not have to pay sales tax because

Massachusetts exempts a person missing two or more limbs from paying sales tax, nor did I have to pay excise tax as a person with a disability. With the purchase of my car Mass Rehab told me that the next steps in the driving process could begin.

First came the bidding process. Mass Rehab took the assessment that contained all the necessary adaptive devices, and sent it out to possible vendors. I was told it would be a few weeks before all the bids would be in, and the lowest bid would win. I was a little concerned that the lowest bid would be the winning one, but I was assured that all the vendors were very capable and the bidding practice was necessary due to budget requirements.

RideAway won my bid. Ride-Away is one of the largest providers of wheelchair vans, vehicle modifications, and adaptive equipment, including hand controls and specialized gas, brake and steering controls. I waited for them to schedule my car for modification. I owned my car for about two months before it was taken in for modification. During this interim, my friends drove my car for me. In preparation for having a car I got the driving manual and began reading it, so I could get my driver's permit again. Other than learning the rules of the road, the manual taught me two important rules regarding disability. First, I was allowed to have handicapped plates on my car, and also I could have a placard for when my car was parked. As a person with a disability, I did not need to adhere to time limits for parking, and if I parked at a meter I did not need to pay.

The car was ultimately modified to fit my needs. I had switches and buttons situated for my reach, and an alternate steering system that allowed me to drive with my left foot. This was an exciting experience for me. I had always dreamed of learning to drive, but was not sure how it would happen. I remember the first day that I was given the opportunity to drive my car. My mom had driven me out to RideAway. All the adaptions to the car had been made. The Mass Rehab inspector was present, and he wanted me to drive the vehicle to make sure that everything was in place.

This was exciting and nerve-wracking at the same time. I was brought over to the car and I looked at my mom and told her she could not come with me. I was far too nervous to have my mom in the car with me. Bill, the man who had installed all the adaptations, got in the car with me. At first I didn't touch the gas pedal. Luckily, we were on a little bit of an incline. I steered the car as I was meant to do, and used the brake a little bit, until we got to the bottom of the incline. Bill looked at me and told me that now I had to use the gas pedal. I looked back at him and said, "Okay", and gently put my foot on the gas. It was a short drive... just around the parking lot, but to me it was far longer. It represented a new chapter in my life. Driving gave me opportunities I had only imagined were possible. I didn't bring the car home that day because it was scheduled to be towed to my house. I was given the name and number of the gentleman who would be teaching me to drive. In June 2001, I went for my license test. I remember telling the officer that I was nervous, and he said he was more comfortable driving with me than he had been with anyone else that day. Within an hour I received my driver's license. My life changed. Getting places was easier and my knee pain became more manageable. Driving also gave me an independence I had never had before. I could go anywhere now, and did!

Chapter 9
Front Page News

Change

Change is in us,
change is around us,
change is because of us.

In us we hold the power.
The intent of our change is within…
we only need to let it loose.

Around us, power is everywhere.
Our intent impacts the change.
We only need to visualize it.

Our power makes the change.
Where do you see yourself going?
Let it loose, visualize it, and it happens.

The change is starting.
The change can be small or large.
The change can pass you by.

Look within yourself.
Open the doors to change.
Close the doors of fear.

Harness the power within.
Harness the power around.
Harness the power because of us.

The energy is growing; hold it.
Mold the energy with intent.
Go forward with it.

Change, power, energy
is in us…
is around us…
is because of us.

When I was a kid my cousin practiced martial arts, and he showed me some of the kicks. I found it fascinating, yet it was almost twenty years before I started my own martial arts training. You often find the best things in life when you are not looking. One cold winter morning while I was at a coffee house in Flagstaff, a flyer for a martial arts school caught my eye. How nice to do something besides work and school. Over the next three years I made good friends at "The Sleeping Lion, and learned important skills. The instructors were open- minded and not at all fazed by my disability. My teachers were thoughtful and added modifications for me. Because I had no arms they helped me learn to use what I do have, and we added more kicks to the routine. This martial arts school also had a variety of disciplines, which gave me a good understanding of what was best for my body structure.

When I left Flagstaff, I also left martial arts. I moved back home, and it was two years before I got involved with martial arts again. East coast martial arts schools were very different from those in the west. My previous school taught many forms of martial arts in one place. Back at home I had to experiment at several schools, but ultimately came to the realization that Tae Kwon Do was the best fit for me. I walked through the doors of Bruce McCorry's Martial Arts and realized it would be the right thing. Before arriving for my introductory class, I spoke with a woman named Sandra. She asked me about my martial arts experience and I told her the details about what I had done in Arizona. She offered me information about what their school did and described their curriculum. At some point during the conversation I did tell her that I had a disability. I don't remember exactly how I described it to her, but I am pretty sure I told her that I had no arms but had hands attached to my shoulders. She did not seem fazed by this, we chose a day for my introductory class and I was excited to begin.

I was concerned that it had been such a long time since I had practiced martial arts, when I walked into the school I felt comfortable immediately. There were a number of people in the lobby, but I quickly found Sandra. I put out my hand right away, to give her a nice handshake. We spoke a little bit and then she brought me into the main room. Since then, many interesting conversations about my first day have been shared between my martial arts friends and I. Apparently, when I arrived in the busy lobby people were a little shocked and immediately dispersed, unsure of how to react to me. Sandra told me much later that the staff thought my call had been a crank call, and people were more than a little surprised that I actually showed up.

My first class was exhilarating. I had so much fun, and it was not that difficult, in the scheme of things. I made it through the full length of the class, despite my worries that I might not be able to handle it. I had a tour of the school, got to know some of the students, and before I left that night, I had signed up for classes. Little did I know that my choice to engage in martial arts would change my life.

From the moment I arrived at Bruce McCorry's Martial Arts School I felt at ease. There were no judgments, no assumptions, and the space was welcoming. My instructors were terrific about accommodating my needs whenever it became necessary. They have never changed anything without consulting me first. I went at my own pace, and they never questioned me.

Many people have asked me what the hardest thing is that I have done in martial arts. Without hesitation, it has been the jumping. Balancing is also extremely challenging for me.

I was born without kneecaps, and my knees bow out, which makes jumping and balancing difficult. I entered Bruce McCorry's as a green belt student. It took some time for me to learn the curriculum at McCorry's, the main difference being that Master McCorry saw no reason that I should not use my hands.

I continue to feel very involved in Bruce McCorry's Martial Arts. We do Tae Kwon Do all the time, which means that I do not need to sit down as often as I did at my first school. My instructors assume that I will take part in any activity that is going on. They know that if I need help, I will ask. I think the biggest accommodation that's ever been made for me when performing martial arts is that I generally take private lessons when I am learning to use weapons.

When the day came to test for my purple belt, I was nervous. I came in early to practice, and stayed late. In the end it went really well. I remembered just about everything that was expected of me. At the end of testing, I was exhausted and my knee hurt a great deal. I took a few days off, and remember getting a call from Sandra because the instructors were alarmed that I had not come back to class after the test. When I returned to class I found out that I had earned my purple belt!

As time went on, I took classes three or sometimes four times a week. I came to class with a positive attitude and did the best I could. I paid attention to my knees, and when they hurt I rested. Master McCorry, Ms. Sandra, and the other instructors all got to know my abilities and understood when I needed to take a break. They also knew when I was just being lazy. Before long I was a brown belt in Tae Kwon Do. Part of the curriculum was that we were required to teach, so I started coming to the children's class on Tuesday evenings. It was incredibly rewarding to be able to do this with the youth. Teaching helped me master my own curriculum, and I was both teacher and student.

Since I have been at McCorry's Martial Arts I have participated in two competitions. First, I went to a competition in New Hampshire where I competed in breaking and forms. I did not do well, but that being said, I continued, I did not stop. My motto was: just keep going. My first competition helped me gain confidence. I had never performed with so many people watching. My second competition was a different story. I competed in weapons and in forms. In my weapons division I was the only contestant, and therefore I got a gold medal. In my forms division there were 12 of us, and I was thrilled when I was awarded third place.

I never dreamed about becoming a black belt in martial arts. I was focused on enjoying myself and learning more and becoming more proficient. Martial arts has always been about the experience. It is about improving myself to be the best I can possibly be. I have never given any thought to what belt color I was or what belt color I could be. I was more than a little surprised when I received paperwork telling me that I should start to prepare for my black belt test. This was the first time since the first test at Bruce McCorry's that I was worried about performance. Students do not attempt black belt t if they are not ready. I received my test sheet and started to go over everything that I would need to know. As the test date grew closer I got more excited. There were also a lot of other things going on for me because the media had picked up my story, as will be described shortly. Then, when the final day actually came I was a bit nervous, as I was not sure what the assessment was going to include. I figured I would just do the best that I could do. It turned out to be an amazing experience, and it was probably the hardest physical event I have ever attempted. It was three and a half to four hours of exercise, and that was huge for my body. I succeeded, and although the next day I could barely move, it was worth it. I had accomplished something I never imagined I could do.

In April, 2010, I had the opportunity to go on an amazing vacation with my childhood friend. We went to Punta Cana, an all-inclusive resort in the Dominican Republic. I had the most relaxing vacation of my life, spent with Danielle, my oldest and dearest friend. There was a small group of us celebrating Danielle's important anniversary. We had endless hours of relaxation, swimming, and conversation. We were celebrating 10 years of her being free from cancer. When I came home, I had no idea how my life was about to change.

Sandra had been trying to reach me while I was in the Dominican Republic. Apparently, the people at McCorry's had a conversation about how I was an inspiration to so many of them through the years. They contacted the local paper, informing them that in just a couple of months I would be going for my black belt. I agreed to be interviewed. A reporter from the Salem Evening News interviewed me about my life. Master McCorry and Ms. Sandra were also involved in the conversation, and the newspaper filmed our martial arts class and took a few pictures. I had forgotten to ask the reporter what section the story would be in, so we all my friends and family flipped through the entertainment and sports sections every day, guessing where the story might be. Six days later I was walking to work at the Salem District Courthouse when one of the court officers looked up at me, smiled said, "I saw you on the front page of the Salem News this morning. Your story is amazing." He handed me the paper and sure enough, there was a picture of me with my nun-chucks, right on the front page. I was a little giddy. I grabbed the paper and went up to the office to read the story. Throughout the day people came by to congratulate me, but nothing prepared me for what happened next.

My story went viral both nationally and internationally. At this time, I had no television or Internet at my house, so I needed to rely on others in order to see this media frenzy around my life. At 6:00 AM on a Wednesday morning, my dad told me that a radio station wanted to interview me "right now." He assured me that if I was not interested it would be okay, but they were fascinated by my story and wanted to ask me some questions. Since I was already awake, I might as well talk to the radio station. As a result of the initial publicity Channel 5, Channel 7, and Fox news, all of which wanted to interview me, contacted me. My sisters called to tell me that had googled me and the number of links continued to multiply. My story was being translated into languages all over the world.

All the media attention blew me away. It was bigger than me, bigger than my story alone. I was receiving letters at the martial arts school and emails on Facebook. My story helped others all over the world. It was this realization that made me aware of my responsibility to share my life story. I have always wanted to make a difference and I here was my opportunity to give back. With the hope to inspire others, I began my journey toward motivational speaking. I felt it was my responsibility to share all that I had learned.

Chapter 10
Accepting Myself

Boom!

goes the beat of one drum.
It vibrates my body to the core.
Deep inside I realize
I am home.

I step into the moss that circles the fire.
The area beneath my feet is soft and pads my steps.

The drums beat and rhythm in the dance begins
Round the fire we go
Sounds echo the dancers find their paths

The paths are many:
Trance, Laughter, Focus,
Pain, Release, Innocence, and Wisdom.

The energy of the inner circle is high All the pathways are in motion.
The outer circle holds the container giving to the needs of the many.
The two circles act as one, nourishing one another

The dance and music pause. The voice starts slowly, then rises.
The chance has arrived.
The energy holds the circle as the dance continues
Slowly the chat gives way to the music, the drums return,
and the dance continues.

The Seva gives to all the parts,
nourishing the container to allow the energy to continue.

Boom! goes the beat of one drum.

I am home!

*W*hen I moved back to Massachusetts after graduate school, it was not long before I sought out a spiritual space. I went to the Unitarian Universalist Church with my mom and learned that there was a ritual planned for Samhain, which is a festival marking the end of the harvest season and the beginning of winter or, the "darker half" of the year. I remember hearing the drums and putting myself right in the front row. There was smoke as part of the ritual, which was making me cough a little. One of the drummers looked at me and said that perhaps I might move farther away so that I did not cough. I replied that it would put me farther away from the drums, and he smiled at me. I could hardly have guessed right then that I had made a really good friend with that small comment.

During coffee hour I got to know Daniel and Christine, and this budding friendship brought me to my tribe, a community of people with similar spiritual paths. It would be almost two months before I arrived at the Drum and Dance community in Cambridge, Massachusetts. I was told there would be drumming, dancing, singing, and friends. It seemed like a wonderful place to go, so without a second thought I asked what time I should be ready. When I arrived at the space it felt so welcoming that I knew I was home. It was one of the first times in my life that I attended a public event and was not stared at or questioned. In no time I had met many of the regular members, and shortly thereafter, I was considered a regular member as well. There were many firsts when I joined this community, and one thing stood out: acceptance! My abilities were never questioned at any time I was engaged in dancing or drumming.

I clearly remember dancing around the drum circle. I had never thought of myself as a dancer, and had on many occasions been self-conscious about the way my body moved, although I had never shared that feeling with anyone. The first night I was at Drum and Dance I felt different, and

I stepped onto the dance floor feeling the beat of the drum, and actually enjoyed myself. I danced without any self-consciousness and lost myself in the music. This community encouraged me to try drumming and chanting. An unexpected gift was an opportunity to begin fire spinning. This was the beginning of my journey to find my spiritual self.

Dancing became a beautiful thing for me at Drum and Dance. I spent hours dancing around with friends. I remember being intrigued about some of my friends' dancing, because they were belly dancing and I wanted to learn how to do it. I already owned a hip scarf with beautiful jingles that had been given to me as a gift on my first night, and so I began the adventure of learning how to belly dance. I am by no means an expert, but I have learned how to move my body in a graceful way, and I can do a mean shimmy.

The shimmy was a bit challenging at first, mostly because I was trying to move the wrong part of my body. One of my friends broke it down for me, and helped me realize that the movement was more centrally located in the knees than I had realized. As soon as I understood the correct movement, the shimmying was easy. I was like a little kid in a candy store when I finally mastered it, and I ran over to show my friend Daniel. He was sitting down with a few other friends and I interrupted them. With great excitement I looked at Daniel and told him to watch what I had learned, and I proceeded to shimmy. After I showed off my new skill I scampered back onto the dance floor with other friends. Later I learned that my little show and tell was duly noted in my friend's LiveJournal. It seemed he enjoyed the moment as much as I did!

The markings on my body: Scars and Tattoos

Within the first year of my life, I had small cross-shaped scars on my ankles. I have been told that they were needed because of the cut down that was necessary. A cut down is when they have to feed or medicate you through your ankles when you are born. It's common practice for preemies and children with disabilities. These were just the first of my many scars. I have about ten scars on my legs, and all of them are different shapes and sizes. All of these procedures had one common goal: for me to walk without leg braces. As the years passed, my feelings about the scars would change.

At times they were cool because I had more interesting scars than all the boys did. I was able to freak out my older sister, Christine, by making her look at them when they were new. As time went on, however, they did not seem so cool, and I found myself hiding them from the world. My legs were bony, skinny, and scarred because of all of the surgeries I had endured. Most of my social insecurity arose from differences in my legs. Finally, as I ended my teen years I shrugged off the embarrassment I felt about my legs and embraced the scars, knowing that they represented the procedures that gave me the strength to walk on my own. In my early twenties I was offered the chance to cover my scars through plastic surgery, and I refused. These scars were a part of me and I was not going to hide a piece of myself again.

In 2009, I decided to make a mark of my own choosing on my body. I was about to get my first tattoo. Some people supported me, some did not, and others could not understand why obtaining a tattoo appealed to me. The WHY was empowering. Throughout my childhood, others created scars on my legs. I was never asked if I wanted the surgeries that would leave scars on my body, but I never said no, either. I wanted to walk, and that was my only thought. This initial tattoo would come to represent the first time that I had requested a mark on my body of my own free will, and, also for the first time in my life, the mark had nothing to do with being able to walk. It was my choice and that was powerful. The tattoo was a Celtic knot. It had layers of meaning for me: a mark on my body of my own choosing, the earth sign of being a Taurus, and the spirituality that I have found as an adult, which represents the mother, the maiden and the crown.

Two years later I got a second tattoo. It was still about my choice and for me it represented me taking back my body. The tattoo sits right next to one of my scars, and now when you look at my leg, the first thing you see is the tattoo, then you might notice the scar. Interestingly, when I was getting the second tattoo, the feel and vibration of the needles reminded me of having my casts removed as a child. That process was scary and sometimes painful. Now I have a new memory that was about choice, and one that was not frightening or painful. The tattoo is a fire fairy. Its symbolism is about my acceptance of myself as a woman with sensuality. I got this tattoo after I had learned to accept my body and love it truly. It was EMPOWERING! As a woman with a disability this voluntary body transformation has continued to be an amazing experience for me.

Chapter 11
The Way

The eyes move first.

Then the body follows,

The body forms the stance,

The stance allows the flow,

The energy flows through the breath,

The breath calms the body,

The body repeats the motion,

The motion calms the mind,

It all repeats…

The mind, body, and spirit are one.

Korean Documentary

On January 11, 2012, I arrived for my Tae Kwon Do class at Bruce McCorry's Martial Arts and was told that some individuals from South Korea had called and wanted to speak with me. It turns out that there was a "trailer" added to the documentary, "Tae Kwon Do: Unity of Mind, Body, and Life", that featured all of us at McCorry's, and a Korean television station was interested in my story. They wanted to produce a five-part documentary about my life, which would include showing me here in the United States and then track a visit I would take to South Korea. They were very eager and wanted to know immediately if I was willing to participate. As exciting as the opportunity was, I told then that I needed to give serious consideration to this opportunity.

The following day I spoke to my friends, family and co-workers about the proposed trip. I also connected with Andrew, a man I met through the prior documentary, "Tae Kwon Do: Unity of Mind, Body, and Life." I called him because I thought he could give me some advice about this proposal. He stepped right up and said that he would contact the television station for me. Meanwhile, my friends and family were on board and excited for me. I was a bit hesitant, as I wanted to have all the relevant information before I made a decision. Andrew became my agent and had conversations on my behalf, so that I could truly understand what the project would entail. In the end I agreed to the filming, and the Korean film crew was to arrive on Tuesday night, January 17, 2012. At this point I was aware that they wanted to film me in my everyday life with my friends, family, co-workers and Tae Kwon Do family. We were to meet with the film crew Wednesday morning, January 18th, to set up a schedule for the next seven to ten days.

This adventure would require good boundaries and thoughtful reflection on the impact the project would have on the lives of others in my life. As much as the film was about me, it would affect all the people in my life, and I was mindful of this. The first meeting with the Koreans gave me a sense of how different we were from one another. Some of the differences were cultural and others had to do with individual personalities. The meeting provided a better sense of the purpose of the documentary. I learned that the documentary was meant to educate youth about bullying, and offer them inspiration towards self-improvement. The documentary would have four themes: one would be my personal life, including family and friends; the second would cover my professional life, including my work with HAWC., an organization devoted to ending domestic violence, as well as my motivational speaking; the third theme was my Tae Kwon Do accomplishments; and fourth, the upcoming trip to South Korea.

During the meeting we reviewed the schedule for the following week. I spoke to the producer about my commitments at work and what could be filmed there. We designed a schedule that was appropriate for Master McCorry's Martial Arts school, as well. Finally, we discussed how to include my family and friends in the film.

The filming lasted longer than I had expected. For 14 days I had a man following me around with a camera. It was an experience that I'm glad to have had, but I am not sure that I would ever do it again. Two weeks is a long time, but it is not really long enough when someone is trying to fit your life into that time frame. They wanted to see me at work, at Tae Kwon Do, hanging out with my friends, being with my family, visiting my childhood hospital, and doing anything else that seemed interesting. This all needed to happen in two weeks, while I continued to work full-time from Monday to Friday. It was challenging and a little exhausting. There were also logistics that were a bit uncomfortable for me when we were filming. There was a bright light and a microphone that was attached to me. I found it amusing that the filmmakers thought the light was not bright, because they were behind the light and not in front of it.

My friends at work and Tae Kwon Do were really accommodating, which made things easier. I was concerned for all of them and wanted to make sure that they were treated with respect all along the way. I think I had more concern for them than they had for themselves. The filming at work was pretty mundane, as it included meetings and sometimes pictured me at my desk doing paperwork and handling phone calls. The filming at my house was all about simple daily tasks such as eating dinner, doing dishes and preparing to leave the house. Tae Kwon Do was a bit more exciting when it came to filming. As the crew began to film I started to see how the documentary was going to play out. I was filmed along with other martial arts students, and then the crew was interested in holding impromptu informal interviews. They filmed Master McCorry, questioning him along with other students and myself.

Some of the filming was more staged than I had imagined, but capturing the spontaneity of one's life is difficult. Staging requires repetitive action. I had assumed that they would just film each day as it happened, but I was learning that was not the case. This was explained to me as the difference between reality TV and a documentary, which is what we were creating. On the second day there was film of me driving to work and some more office activity. We got to my workplace and I introduced the cameraman to everyone. Then he asked me to go outside and come back in because it was important to film transitions, so I left the office and came back in as if it was first thing in the morning. We captured a meeting with a volunteer, and then the crew interviewed HAWC's executive director. Later in the day, the filmmakers had the opportunity to film me giving a presentation at Salem Hospital about my experiences with the medical field growing up.

I met my parents for dinner that night at my favorite pizza place, Santarpio's in Peabody. My parents and I arrived at the restaurant before the camera crew, so we needed to reenact our arrival. Mom and Dad had laughed when I told them that this might happen because the coming and going was important to film. We sat down and had some casual conversation at first, and then there were some informal interview questions for both of my parents. The filming stopped for a time so we could eat, and at times we repeated stories that Momo, the producer, wanted captured as we talked throughout the evening. Overall, it was a pleasant time.

The following day I had a bit of down time during the filming. A small camera was installed by my desk to capture the everyday things I did. I received confirmation from my friend Misty that we could go to her house for the day. This was a visit that we had hoped to be able to make, as Misty's son has TAR syndrome, as I do. The producer hoped that we would be able to portray my friendship with Misty's family and show the mentoring that had taken place over the past five years. Later I went roller-skating with friends for the second time in 15 years. It was a really fun evening. A few days later, I was filmed roller-skating with friends and family.

Unfortunately, only a few of us were able to go roller-skating for the filming, since there was a virus going around at work. As it turned out, my sister, nephew, dad, and two friends were able to come. When we arrived the rink was already being used for lessons. We filmed for about half an hour. While we were waiting to figure out the filming details, we realized that my roller skating teacher from years before was at the rink giving lessons. I did not get to talk to him because he was teaching, but I did talk to his wife. It was great to catch up with her after so many years. While we were there, the crew interviewed my friends and family, which was fine, but then they tried to interview my former teacher. He listened to their request and politely declined. Since his wife remembered me, she was interviewed for a few minutes. They wanted me to be a part of the interview as well, but I lasted only a few minutes and left, as my legs were tired and I needed to sit down fast!

Skating was a lot of fun and also harder than I remembered, although I suppose that after 15 years of not roller skating it would be difficult for anyone. The way I originally learned to skate involved a kind of scissors movement, which consisted of bringing my feet in and out in a half-circle rotation. This created pressure on my thigh muscles, and when I was skating all the time it was easy. I can't say it feels the same nowadays. I also used to skate with professional skates, and I'm sure that also factored into how easy skating seemed when I was younger. When I was a child I was skating a lot, and I'm sure that made a huge difference in my proficiency.

After I had skated for a little while the producer wanted to hear about skating from my perspective. He put a camera on my head to get the view from the perspective of my eyes. Unfortunately, it was very uncomfortable and distracted me, and within just a minute or two I fell, and man, did it hurt. I fell on the side where my microphone box was attached. Once I was on the floor I realized I needed to find a way to get up, and I was smack in the middle of the rink. This was a problem, as I could not get up off the ground, as I had had as a child. I had learned to get up on one knee with one foot flat on the ground, and then I was able to hop to standing, which would be pretty tricky on skates. Luckily, I had my friends and family with me, and they assisted me to my feet.

The next day we were back to some serious filming. We started with my morning routine, which meant that I needed to "wake up" while the cameraman was shooting. I was in fits of giggles for about five minutes while this was happening. They had me get back into bed and close my eyes, and then they filmed me. Then, when they gave me the go-ahead I had to get up. It was an odd experience. Throughout the filming there were requests that made sense to the producer but did not represent how I actually live day to day. For example, that morning they wanted me to put on the same clothes that I had worn the morning before, to continue filming the morning routine. That would have been fine if we had had more time before my Tae Kwon Do class, but since it had snowed the night before, it was a problem. Even though a documentary was being filmed, I was still living my daily life, and being on time is important to me.

Fortunately, they respected my feelings and that they remained flexible.

The unexpected winter storm that day presented an unplanned opportunity to show me clearing snow off of my car. For most people clearing snow off a car doesn't amount to much, but for a woman with no arms it is rather interesting to watch, since I have had to work out a method to accomplish this task. I currently have a remote starter in my car, which has made winters a lot easier for me. Prior to getting the remote, there have been many times when I needed to find someone to help me open the car door, and that experience taught me that a remote starter was not a luxury, but a necessity for me. Since my hands are not very strong, pulling open a door with lots of snow and ice packed around it is not easy. Now I am able to warm up the car before going outside and getting my snowbrush.

When I first moved home from Arizona my brother-in-law, Mike, gave me the best present ever. It was a snowbrush that was about three feet long and extended to seven or eight feet. This meant that I could fully extend the brush and push the snow off my car fairly easily. The brush also limited how much snow landed on top of me while cleaning the car, which I really appreciate. So I spent a few minutes that morning with my reach- extending snowbrush, clearing off my car before Tae Kwon Do. The producer asked me a number of questions about how I had learned to do this, and if it had been a difficult process. As with most things in my life I explained that this is just how I do things, and some days it can be frustrating and other days it's fine. Then we spent a little time driving down the street in the snow, and finally went off to Tae Kwon Do.

Tae Kwon Do

Tae Kwon Do was the main reason that my documentary and trip to South Korea came, so it stands to reason that there would be a lot of filming showing me practicing Tae Kwon Do. The producer was interested in seeing me during training, and in particular, showing me as I assisted in teaching some of the younger students. He also wanted to show some interviews with my peers and some of the youthful students as well. It was a little awkward having a camera in my martial arts class. Usually, when I went to Tae Kwon Do it was a time I could relax and clear my mind, with no thoughts and no questions, but when someone is preparing a documentary on your life and they're filming you during class there are many questions and many thoughts. Once we got into a little bit of a routine it was more tranquil.

Any night that they were filming, Master McCorry had me do a warm-up for the class. This gave the film crew the opportunity to see me assuming a senior leadership role, as I often did at martial arts. Master McCorry ran his classes in a way that allowed the filming while continuing to meet the needs of all the students in the class, which was very important. He also had us doing many different things so that the film crew saw a variety of movements. Additionally, there were times when I worked individually, breaking wood or performing with weapons. The producer enjoyed observing the different activities, which provided with a well- rounded view of my Tae Kwon Do training. Because the crew was there so often, they saw me do things well sometimes, and at other times, not so well. I broke the board most of the time, but a couple of times I did not. Throughout the different classes many of the students were interviewed, and they were all terrific. I think they actually had a great time participating in the film.

One day we shot one of our regular sparring classes. Sparring is a form of training common to many martial arts and it is the way Tae Kwon Do students prepare for self-defense. Students wear gear to protect themselves from injury and then use the techniques learned in class in a fight. Sparring gives students the opportunity to display their abilities in a safe, controlled competitive environment while still showing respect to their opponent. By this point I had been followed around by a camera for about five days, and the thought of sparring made me happy because I

knew that there was going to be no time for thoughts or questions, and I
really needed a mind break. But before the class started my friends were
asked to place cameras on their heads in order to capture the fighting
from different angles. This made me uncomfortable, since as much as
I understood why the producer would want this, I was looking out for
the other students. After mentioning my discomfort to the producer he
understood and respected my desire which was a great relief to me. Class
was excellent, because we were sparring and moving around quickly and
there was no time for questioning or interviewing. I was free to focus on
Tae Kwon Do, and that really appealed to me. After sparring there were
some questions, but by then I was too tired to care.

The crew continued to interview young students. The first time, it was
more than just an interview. I had a little private class with one student. We
did some forms and combinations and then also went over his weapons.
It was a short lesson, as he had another class to attend. Before returning
to class he smoothly answered the questions they had for him, and then
after he went to class they interviewed his mom. The second student
they interviewed was part of the regular Tuesday class where I regularly
assisted. The interview went really well and I learned that the student had
been bullied at school, as I had. This was something that I had not known
before. She also told me that when I gave a presentation at her school
during the past year it had really made a difference for her to know that I
was bullied when I was a child, and that she was not alone. Hearing that
my presentation had made a difference to her made me feel really good. It
also reminded me of the reason it was so important for me to continue to
tell my story to people both here in the United States and all over the world.
Stories of survival can make such a difference for others when they're
going through hard times. After the interview we stretched, and then there
was a class for her. We did kicking drills during class and I went around
helping with the kicks and with keeping the students focused.

Interviews

Witnessing my story through the eyes of my friends and family was another aspect of the filming that was captivating for me. There was a full day with the family that included interviews and casual activities. As I mentioned previously, we took a trip to Cape Cod to visit with a friend whose child has the same disability as I do. We also paid a visit to Shriners' Hospital for Children, where I spent so much time as a child, and one of my oldest friends was interviewed as well.

Prior to committing to the filming I made a promise to my nephew that I would take him to the Lego store. When the producer requested time with the entire family we were able to turn the visit to the Lego store into a family event. My sister Lisa and her son, Evan, came down from New Hampshire. My sister Christine and her daughter, Georgia, made the trip from Maine. The producer spoke in advance with the manager of the Lego store and they agreed to allow us to film our family as long as they did not include other people who were in the store. This worked out well, as I had told the film crew that this was an event that I was not going to cancel because I wanted to honor my commitment to my nephew.

I told my family to be prepared for random questions, and sure enough, one of the questions that stood out was when they asked about childhood toys. We were in the Lego store, so I guess it made sense to pose a question about what toys I had enjoyed as a child. Otherwise, we just hung out as a family and had fun while we were being filmed. One of the most humorous moments of the day happened when we were all going down the escalator together. It reminded us a little bit of a scene out of "The Brady Bunch". We ended up going up and down the escalator a couple times in order to get a good shot, and of course my father was giving me bunny ears behind my head.

After the enjoyable event at the Lego store with my family, we headed back to my parents' house for lunch. The producer wanted to have some formal interviews with my family, and he interviewed each person separately and asked them many questions about my life. Both of my sisters told me that the hardest question he asked them was what made me so special. For them I was not special at all, I was just their Sheila. My parents had always treated us equally, and my having a disability did not matter to any of us. It was expected that I would do everything that my sisters did, and that was just the way it was for my sisters, my parents, and me. One interesting piece of the interview for my sisters was seeing how different some of their memories were of our childhood. That makes a lot of sense to me. We all remember things differently because of who we are and what our numerical place is in the family. I think for the most part my sisters had a pretty good time being interviewed. At one point they wished they had had an opportunity to redo their conversations, because they didn't feel they were given enough time to think about their answers.

My parents experience with their interview was different from my sisters. My mom had never really spoken to anyone about my childhood before. As I have gotten older I have asked some questions here and there, and with current media attention she and I had had a little bit of a dialogue. My mother always did everything she needed to do to help me succeed. There had been many occasions when doctors had asked her to speak with other families about her experiences, and she had always declined because it was too hard for her to do. Her focus was on helping me succeed, and she felt comfortable that she had succeeded at that, so she never looked back. This would be the first time that she had sat down with a stranger and spoken about my childhood. I knew that it was really difficult for her to do this, and I so appreciated the fact that she was willing to have this conversation on my behalf. I spoke to the producer in advance and explained to him that it was very difficult for my mom to have a discussion about me, and he needed to be very gentle with her, and he was terrific. I cannot say that the interview was easier for Dad, but it was different. My dad and I had had many conversations about my childhood. When I became curious about something I often talked to him about it, because he seemed more comfortable with my questions than Mom did. His interview also gave me a chance to see the softer side of Dad. I know that he's really proud of me because he has told me, and the rest of my family has told me he is proud of me, as well. But to hear some of the things he said about me and actually see how fulfilled my success has made him was really moving.

The interviews with my niece, Georgia, and nephew, Evan, were a bit less formal, as they should be with children. My sisters had told the kids about the documentary and explained that a producer wanted to ask them questions about Auntie Sheila. They were both very sweet. Georgia told the producer that I gave the best hugs. Evan was being his cute little self and when asked what his name was, he told the producer he was busy. After a little coaching from my sister, he talked a little bit, although I think the questions about Auntie Sheila were a little strange for both of them. They have known me their whole lives and do not see me as unusual. I remember when I was on the news a lot and Lisa was showing Evan some of the videos, and he asked her why I was on TV. He didn't understand what was such a big deal about Auntie Sheila. That's because they have been brought up the same way that my sisters and I were brought up as children.

A few months after the filming ended I had an opportunity to look at the interviews with my family and some of my close friends. It was humbling to hear them praise me and share stories about how proud they are of me. It was an emotional experience to watch the videos of the people closest to me. I have never tried to be an inspirational person, I have just always focused on being myself and finding a way to succeed.

During the filming, we got to visit the family that I had been mentoring, and with whom I had become close friends. I had felt a connection to Misty and her family for about five years. As I have written in a previous chapter, Shriners' Hospital for Children had introduced us after Misty's son Michael was born with TAR syndrome. The interview provided us with an opportunity to join Michael at his Kung Fu class, and visit with the family at their house afterwards.

Michael's Kung Fu class was totally inclusive. The instructors taught the core material to all the students and then worked with each of them individually to improve their skills. Michael's participation in class is 100%. He lined up with the rest of the students and performed the exercises while adapting the skills as needed. His instructors had worked with him independently to assist him in figuring out how to modify each exercise. It was amazing for me to see such an inclusive classroom, where instructors worked with each student so he or she could benefit to the greatest degree. The inclusivity at Bruce McCorry's is why I choose to study there; however in my experience that has not been the norm. During one class at Michael's school I had the joy of being the guest of honor and joining in their routine. My style of martial arts is Tae Kwon Do, Kung Fu also works well for me. I have to say, it was quite an experience.

After the class Michael and I did some training together with the instructors, who spoke about how their teaching style was made to fit Michael's abilities. Then Michael demonstrated several of his skills. I got to see Michael's version of a pushup, which is similar to mine. I also was able to share some tips with Michael about using rolling in his routine to gain more power with his kicks. We finished the instruction with a kicking routine between Michael and me that we tweaked just a bit so that it was a good fit for our abilities.

After a morning of Kung Fu it was time for lunch. Just before lunch I watched Michael walk with his braces for the first time. This was a remarkable experience for me, for as much as I saw that walking was amazing for him, I also understood and empathized with his struggle. The braces were uncomfortable and he had not quite mastered them, so he still needed help walking. He had a bit of a "moment" and just wanted to take them off. I went over to him told him that I understood what it's like to wear braces, since I had to wear my braces every single day at school when I was kid. He looked at me and said, "Wow! I only have to wear them on Tuesdays and Thursdays."

After the braces were put away, we played some video games. Michael was excited to show me a game that he played very often, and he wanted me to play it with him. I found myself telling him that I am not really good at video games because of my hands… and then I stopped speaking. I thought for a moment and realized I was about to tell this young man that my hands were too short to play video games, when his hands are just like mine. I looked back at him and asked if he could show me how he played, because I was not very good at it, and he smiled. Before I knew it Michael was rolling down the hallway a mile a minute, yelling for me to come into the den. I followed and very shortly he had me playing video games with him. He showed me how he used his chin to maneuver the joystick on the controller and then use his hand for the buttons. That process actually works very well, and soon I was getting the hang of it. Michael was much faster and better at the game than I, but for the first time I found playing a video game a little easier.

This is an example of how every relationship in your life can provide a learning experience. Meeting Michael and his family gave me an opening to be a mentor, because I had gone through so many similar experiences before they did. At the same time, I was learning from them as well.

Taking part in making a film also showed me how I had positively impacted the life of one of my friends. When I was about 10 years old, on a swing at a playground, I met several members of a family. As the years progressed I became very close friends with Danielle. We were campground friends, which meant that we saw each other about three times a year, at holiday times. Our friendship continued and became strong, and whenever we saw each other it was as though we had just been together yesterday. Since Danielle has known me from the time I was 10, she was there with me as I grew up struggling with daily activities, and also when people annoyed me. She saw me at my best and my worst, and she knew that I never let anything bring me down.

When Danielle was 14 she was faced with a cancer diagnosis. I remember receiving a phone call from her when I was a sophomore in college. She told me about all the aches and pains in her hip that were caused by her cancer. Sitting on the couch listening to her, I had no idea what to say to her. I never had someone that close to me have to deal with anything like this. I did what I thought I could do best, which was to continue to be her friend as I always had been and always would be. I did not know at the time that our friendship would be one of the factors that helped her survive her battle with cancer.

During her treatments we stayed in contact. When we got a chance to see each other we did everything we had always done, but our conversations were different because of everything that was going on with her. We often talked about how to get through difficult things. I remember visiting her once just before a holiday weekend. Her family had plans to go to the campground we knew growing up, but unfortunately, Danielle's blood count went down and she needed to go into the hospital for a transfusion. She tried to convince me that I should go with her mom and she would go to the hospital with her dad. This seemed absurd to me. I told her that there was no way I was leaving her to go to the campground when she was going to the hospital. She tried to insist, because the hospital was not a pleasant place. I looked at her and reminded her that I had spent long hours in a hospital growing up and I knew exactly what they were like. I also knew that having a friend go to the hospital with you is a very nice thing.

Sitting in my kitchen almost 15 years later, Danielle brought tears to my eyes when she told me that my friendship really helped her survive her cancer. She had seen everything that I had gone through as a child, and felt that if I could make it through, it so could she. Interestingly, she was an inspiration to me through her ordeal, as well. I remember being frustrated with college and with other daily things. Then I would stop myself and realize that one of my closest friends had cancer and I was the one complaining. It helped me learn to put things in perspective. Friendship is a wonderful thing, especially when it is circular, with each person contributing to the relationship equally.

Looking back on the documentary experience, I am glad I did it. The overall message was excellent, although the entire experience was not easy. I had two or three people with me every day for fourteen days. Even though it was not every moment of the day, when the crew was not there I still knew we had more filming to do soon. They also wanted to be able to film as many parts of my life as possible in two weeks, which meant that I needed to plan things and see if friends and/or family were available to participate. I was also in the middle of planning a volunteer training at work, and as I had never done that before I was under a lot of stress. It was a tough schedule and I was constantly worrying about how my friends and family were feeling about doing the interviews and having random cameras in their faces as we were engaged in an activity. We filmed at Tae Kwon Do five different times, and I did not want that to have a negative effect on the other students. My usual stress relief at Tae Kwon Do was not an option because I always had to be on point for the camera. It was a huge event in my life and I am happy it turned out as it did.

My trip to South Korea

The United States filming ended mid-day on January 31, 2012, which meant I had two and a half days to take care of all my responsibilities at work and get myself packed before I left for South Korea. At 5:30 on

Thursday night I shut down the computer in my office and looked over at my friend and said, "I'm going to South Korea tomorrow, wow!" It hit me for the first time, mostly because I was so focused on making sure things were organized at work. I went home to finish packing and got to bed early. I had to be up at 3:00 a.m. to catch a shuttle to the airport in order to make my 6:00 a.m. flight to JFK airport in New York.

I must say that 3:00 a.m. is far too early to be up, even when you are in bed by 9 p.m. the night before. Still, I got up and got ready, and by 3:45 my shuttle was at the front door. It was a quick ride into Logan Airport, since there were not that many people on the road. Once I was at the airport, things went quickly. I checked in and waited for wheelchair assistance. This was going to be a long day, so I was going to limit my walking. A number of years ago I started using wheelchair assistance at airports as a means of taking care of myself. On such a long flight, I had no way of knowing how my legs were going to feel when I arrived half way around the world.

I flew Korean Air in the largest plane I had ever seen. It was two stories high and was referred to as an airbus. We had coach tickets, but the accommodations were nicer than I expected. I had an individual TV, so I could watch what I liked, when I liked. Everyone was also given little bags containing slippers, toothpaste and a toothbrush. I have never been fed so much on a plane, and the food was pretty good, too. The flight was far too long… 15 hours… but I read, watched movies, listened to music, slept a few different times, played video games and had time to sit and think. By the time we landed I was done with the plane and happy to be on land. My legs were a bit sore and swollen, despite my efforts to walk around on the plane, and my feet barely fit in my shoes. I was happy that I had a wheelchair reserved. As we exited the plane the reality that I had traveled half way around the world set in. There was little to no written or spoken English around me. We were brought to get our luggage and then went on to customs, and I was totally lost. Eventually, the Korean film crew met us.

After 15 hours on a plane I was sore and a little disoriented and here I was, on film again. They wanted my impressions of Korea, but I did not have much to say as I had only had seen the airport.

It was about a 45-minute ride to Hotel M, where we were staying. Seoul is a pretty modern city with many people, businesses, buildings, and traffic, and as it is with most cities, no parking. The hotel I stayed at was very nice. There was a little walk-in area in my room, where the guest would take off their shoes and put on the slippers that were provided. The floor was heated! There were the usual hotel amenities, but the bathroom setup was a bit different. There was a second set of slippers to change into when entering there. It took a little bit of time to figure out the arrangement, because everything was written in Korean characters. The shower stall drained out onto the floor instead of a self-contained space. I figured this out after soaking two towels, as I usually leave things on the floor. I later realized that this was a typical setup in Korea, and became aware of some of the small cultural differences between our two countries. I made it to 9 pm on my first night and fell fast asleep.

My first full day was tightly scheduled. The first stop was Kukkiwon, the headquarters of Tae Kwon Do. I had been told that they were having an event that day and I was invited. It was not until that morning that I realized that this event was the weekly testing that took place for students in Seoul. Students did not get tested at their local schools; rather, everyone came here. The place was packed with at least five hundred people. When we first arrived we met with a number of the Masters, and then I interacted with some of the students. Students lined the hallways practicing, and the testing space was huge. Watching the students demonstrate the forms that I recognized were comforting. I was lost in the spoken language around me, but I understood the language of Tae Kwon Do.

Once I was settled in I realized that I was scheduled to demonstrate my skills on the open floor in front of everyone. This was just a little bit of a scary and overwhelming experience. Before I knew it I was changing into my Do-Bulk (uniform) in order to perform my hyung (form). I had some time to practice in the hallway, which was helpful, as I was so nervous. As I was trying to practice, the camera was staring back at me, and I told the cameraman he had to leave. I needed to get centered, and having a camera in my face was not working for me. He understood and let me be, asking if he could film me practicing a little later, and I agreed. The preparation only lasted a few more minutes and then I was called to the floor. Since I know little or no Korean, an interpreter was brought to the floor, and there was a lot of gesturing to get me to the proper place. Once there, I waited my turn to be brought forward. There were many people there and there was a three ring setup to accommodate all the testing, so there was a lot of activity. When I came forward things were brought to a stop. A man introduced me… at least I assume he did, as it was all in Korean, and then I heard, "chariot" (attention), "kyung-nae" (bow), "jhoon-bee" (ready) and "she-jae" (start). Thank you, Bruce McCorry's Martial Arts, for teaching me these important Korean words.

It all went fast, as forms do not take very long. I was presented with a new uniform and another black belt. When I was done I thanked the Masters. Then I did some practicing in the hallway for the camera. Following this, I posed for pictures with everyone. People were coming up to me from every direction. It was a trip. Next, we went for lunch on the grounds and I had my first Korean meal. It was pretty good, except for the spicy cabbage, kim chi, which I later learned is Korea's national food. I also impressed everyone as I used chopsticks to eat lunch. Thank you, Mr. K's, Asian-African class. Then we went to a museum upstairs which held all things relating to Olympic Tae Kwon Do. It also had pictures of a less modern Kukkiwon.

During my stay, the film crew organized some opportunities for me to meet with and speak to Korean youth. The first group was the Scouts. It was interesting to learn that there are boy scouts and girl scouts in Korea. I was a participant in the day's event, and my role was to speak to the scouts about my life, in terms of both bullying and Tae Kwon Do.

I began my speech by saying "Annyeonghaseyo" which is "hello" in Korean. It was one of the few Korean words that I knew, and I thought it would be polite to say it to the audience. To my surprise I got a great deal of applause. I spoke to the students and their families for about half an hour. There were questions for me, and afterwards, photos were taken. Overall, it was an amazing day. I was able to meet with families, and hopefully, make a difference.

My second full day in Korea was all about Tae Kwon Do. I had the pleasure of meeting with the president of Kukkiwon, who gave me a Letter of Commendation … In Recognition of Outstanding Contribution to the Development and Dissemination of Tae Kwon Do. It was a great honor. Following this, we visited the open area where the testing had taken place the day before, and did a bit of filming. I had to do a little self- advocacy with the film crew, as they wanted me to walk around and then stand still for about ten minutes. I had to explain that standing still for several minutes and constantly having to walk around was really hard on my legs. Sometimes it's very frustrating when people ask me to do things that are clearly difficult for me, but then I stop and realize that people are not familiar with my limitations. This is one of the reasons that self- advocacy is so important for me. My next stop was a local Tae Kwon Do school that had students with and without disabilities.

I was barely in the door when I was asked to speak. I introduced myself and said hello, and then took a minute to set down my jacket. Then I spoke a bit about my life and my experience with Tae Kwon Do. The school had planned a demonstration for me exhibiting forms, breaking, and sparring. Then I was asked to perform and I did some kicking drills, breaking, nunchucks and sparring. Later we had lunch and talked. A few of the students tried to teach me some Korean words, and I tried to teach them some English. There were interviews with the Master, some students, and myself.

There was also a reporter and cameraman from a local TV station, who wanted to capture the day with me. There was a second class that I joined, and that class was for students with disabilities. I entered the class as they were doing a basic form that I was able to learn quickly, and it was lot of fun.

That evening we had plans to eat Korean Barbecue at a local restaurant. By the time we got there I was hungry and cranky. The film crew was taking forever to get going and it was cold outside. I went into the restaurant and tried to get them to move along, but that did not work. They needed the coming and going. I went outside, annoyed, and then came back in, hoping to eat soon. The next thing I knew, the cameraman was in my face again, asking me what I thought of the place. I said it was nice. I was asked if that was all I had to say. I responded that I was sore, tired, cranky, and hungry, and I would prefer to talk more after I had eaten. At the time I thought to myself that I was certain my grouchy comment would make it into the film, and it did. Dinner was quick to arrive and I was given kim chi again. I immediately put it aside, knowing that I did not like it from having tried it the day before. Momo, the producer who filmed me in the United States, met us for dinner, which was excellent. He was the person who taught me to say "Annyeonghaseyo", and he told me he thought my pronunciation was very good now. All in all, dinner was a very nice experience.

On the third and final day we started out with a visit to the Tae Kwon Do Promotion Federation. This group funded the first documentary in which I had taken part. There was a short business meeting, during which I was asked to write a brief message to the Korean people. I was also asked to be a speaker at the World Youth Tae Kwon Do summer camp, an invitation that I accepted. We watched a video about the Tae Kwon Do Park that is being built in Korea. It was an outstanding meeting, and they gifted me with some really nice things, including a framed picture for my Master, a new uniform, a spoon set, and a calendar.

That afternoon we did some sightseeing. We tried to go to the royal palace, but it was closed on Tuesdays. However, we did get to look around the front part of the grounds and take some pictures. Then we went to the highest point in Seoul and got to see the whole city, which was beautiful. There I learned about the "locks of love". People come to this place, set down locks on the fence, and write messages to their loved ones. I left a lock for my family. Later we went to the largest outdoor market in Seoul. I was looking forward to buying a necklace for myself. The market place was lovely, although it was a bit cold. Later in the day I met up with a reporter from a Tae Kwon Do newspaper and did a short interview.

On my last night we went to a lovely restaurant. One of the interesting things that happen while eating in Korea is that one does not order individual dishes. It seems that things come as an appetizer would in America, and then everyone eats from every dish. We ordered pizza that was very different from what we have here. There was no sauce and it was on a kind of dough that is not similar to ours, but it was good. Dinner was tasty, and there was no filming! After we ate I joined Momo for drinks and dessert. It was nice to see him again, as I had spent so much time with him while he was filming me in Massachusetts. Momo walked me back to the hotel and wished me a good flight home. I went up to my room to pack. I was having a hard time fitting everything in the suitcase, as I had been given a number of things as gifts over the last three days.

The flight home was just as nice as it had been on the way to Korea, and I was on the same two-story plane. Going home was a bit shorter… 12 hours instead of 15. Unfortunately, it felt much longer, probably because I slept less than I had on the first flight. Eventually, we landed at JFK airport, and then it was a short flight home to Boston. I did have a few hours at JFK before boarding for Boston. Once I had gone through customs I texted home and got my messages from my family. My sister Lisa and I talked for a while about my trip and all the things that had been going on while I was gone. I had had a wonderful journey, but it felt so good to be home!

Overall Thoughts

When I reflect on my trip to Korea, I'm glad that I had the opportunity to go. There are some things that I wish had been different. It would have been better if there had been more translating available to me. It seemed that there was an interpreter only when I specifically needed to be part of a conversation. I am aware that this was probably because I was being filmed, but nonetheless, it was frustrating. I understood the words for hello, thank you and Sheila. That was much too little. The worst part was hearing my name all the time and not understanding what was being said. I spent my childhood aware that people were whispering things about me, and even though this was not the same situation, it brought back some of those unpleasant memories. I was in Korea for three days and was exasperated the entire time because I couldn't understand what was being said. From this experience I have developed a new respect for people coming to America without knowing the language or the culture. Also, I wish I had a friend with me. Andrew was there as an agent and he made sure that things went smoothly, but it would have been more fun to share this experience with a friend or family member.

Chapter 12
Disability Not!

Believe

Believe the possible.
It will happen.
Believe the impossible.
It will happen.

The ability to achieve and succeed is within all of us.
The power of belief is held strong in some,
and amazing dreams come true.

Start simple and let it grow.
Accept the setbacks and let it grow.

Embrace what you receive.
All that is meant to happen occurs when you believe.

I choose to believe.
I started simple and it has grown beyond my imagination.

Stand beside me and choose to believe.
I believe that you can succeed.

Side-by-side we all can hold the power of belief...
And bring it to the many.

*M*ost the time I forget that I have a disability. To some people that would seem a bit odd, but to my friends and family it makes a lot of sense, simply because they frequently forget my disability too.

In early December I experienced pain in my knee, so I could not go shopping with my mom. My dad turned around and said, "Well, you should just get one of those scooters and go shopping." I looked at him and said, "Those do not work so well if you don't have arms". He stopped, looked at me and said, "Oh, I forgot." Other people in my life have made the following comments about times when they forgot that I am different:

"I remember hitting my funny bone so hard it brought tears to eyes. I turned to you and said, "Don't you hate when that happens?" Then I realized what I said and we laughed about it. I have a ton of those memories. I never think of you as disabled more times than not I have to remember that you may need help. We were shopping and you were trying to get your wallet out of your purse and the salesperson looked at me and said, "Aren't you going to help her?" I looked at her like she was crazy and said she is fine she doesn't need any help. Then there were the times growing up when you would ask me to get you something and I would say get it yourself then I would remember and, oh yeah, that may be a little hard with no arms. I am so proud of you for all you have done and not just because of your disability."
- Lisa

"Sometimes when I do something with my feet, I say I am just like Auntie Sheila and you are good at karate."
- Evan

"You came to meet Tony and go wedding dress shopping with me. You two were watching TV and you had the remote at your feet. He grabbed it and changed the channel. You were so mad! He said it was not like I took it from your hands or anything, and you looked at him like, DUH!"
- Julie

"Wait... you have a disability? I do not THINK of you that way, so it struck me as weird that you stated that... I always think of you as YOU... this powerful force of nature who storms in with this big grin."
- Jane

"That time at Victoria's Secret"... Every time I suggested something you had to remind me that you had to be able to get into it on your own. No complicated clasps, straps, etc. But I kept picking the wrong things because I thought they were cute. Then we ended giggling our butts off in the dressing room as you tried to make things work."
- Jackie

"I always just knew you as YOU. I think I've had moments a few times where I have totally forgotten, but things come up and I am like, 'Huh, ok' The first time was when Kinz first met you, and we stopped and talked with you, and you very kindly answered every single one of her questions. After you spoke she was like, 'Ok, got it.'"
- Sarah

"When you were in my car you kept having to ask me to help you with the seatbelt because I kept forgetting. I am so used to you buckling the seatbelt in your own car."
- Zayda

" When we were in a hot tub together at a friend's house, just chatting away for about 30 minutes about life, sex, religion, heartbreak... and then I tried to hand you a drink because you asked for one!!! LOL!!! It took me a minute to realize why you had not taken it from me, until you hopped up on the side of the hot tub!"
- Kathleen

"I have to admit, I have a hard time thinking of you as "handicapped" or "disabled" because I still remember Corde saying, 'I like Sheila. She can put my shoes on with her feet! That means she can do more than other people. I can not put someone's shoes and socks on with my feet.' Even now, Corde still says, "How is she 'disabled' when she's able to do so much cool stuff that 'able-bodied' people can't do? I think she must be 'extra-abled'. Either that or she gets extra credit for having better monkey toes than mine.'"
- Erica

"The first time I met you I had heard stories about you, and not one of them included your not having arms. Then, when you arrived, you bounded in with more energy than a speeding Mack truck and said, 'You're Jackie, give me a hug.' I have to admit I was taken aback that no one had mentioned a lack of arms, but now I know why it never occurred to anyone. We all forget all the time."
- Jackie

"When I was living in Worcester and working at Friendly's you came in with Jackie and Katie. My boss asked which one of you was my girlfriend. I said, 'She's the one on the left...the one with no arms'. She was mortified and said, 'Don't say that, she might hear you', and I responded, 'She knows she doesn't have arms.' I think she was even more disturbed by that comment, but I didn't really view it as a handicap because you refused to view yourself that way."
- Dev

"At my workshop, you went to use the restroom. After the door closed and you stood there in the dark, you asked where the light switch was and I told you it was a pull chain over your head. Then I heard you say, '.... oh.'"
- Kaye

"I had put your drinks in the fridge and a short time later you asked if you could reach them. I said, 'Yeah, you can, they are on the top shelf'. You got up to go to the kitchen and Jackie and I followed. When I got there you were standing on one leg trying to reach the top shelf. I wrapped my arms around your stomach, picked you up, and then you could reach the bottles with your foot. You grabbed onto one of the bottles with your toes and pulled it down. I put you down up on the ground and you grabbed your drink. I said, 'See? You reached it!'"
- Brian H

"What comes to mind is how all the servers in Korea tried to give you forks, and I was thinking, 'That's really weird', then considered that it might seem to them that chopsticks would be a challenge, but I knew better."
- Danielle

"There was the time at the Museum of Science's Egypt exhibition
when you said you could not walk like an Egyptian and I
asked you why and you waved your hands at me."
- Michelle T

" I have to say I really like your new shirts, but every time
I look at them and realize that they're short-sleeved, I get
concerned that your arms are getting cold. Whoops,
I guess that's not really a problem is it?"
- Jessie

"I remember when Emma was first born. You came over
to the house to meet her and asked could you hold her. I
remember asking you how you would do that. You responded,
'With my feet'. And of course, I was, like, 'Oh, okay here you go'.
I handed her off to you without another thought."
- Jamie

"You were in a bathing suit top and towel and we were coming out
of the bathrooms. A young boy coming down from the pool said
something like, 'Where are you hiding your arms?!' and you just
explained, like you always do, 'I was born without arms', and he
kinda stared, maybe asked 'why', and you gave more detail, then
we went back up to the pool. I don't remember the conversation
because I was thinking, 'That was so rude!! How could he just say
that and stare that way at a stranger he doesn't know?!' It made
me so angry! You were very calm, though, and shrugged it off.
I was probably 10-12 and the boy was probably 8ish. Your
response has always stuck with me."
- Kelly

"Daniel and I were at your new home for a party and we wanted tea.
So we put the kettle on and started looking for teacups ...
in the upper cabinets where most people keep them.
As we were going through them, we noticed they were all empty.
I remember thinking, 'Wow, I need to buy Sheila some dishes'.
Then I remembered that you keep them low ... and why.
And I had to laugh at myself & shake my head in disbelief
at not remembering where you would keep your dishes."
- Gisela

"I remember that we would be out driving and you would start to park and I would always forget that you could park in the handicapped parking spots."
Jen H

"I needed to go car shopping and so I asked if you could take me. After not finding anything we got back in the car ready to go. You put the car into reverse and I remember saying, 'Sheila, you need to…' and then I was quiet. You said, 'No, finish… I want to know', with a bit of laughter. I said, 'Put your hand on the wheel.' You giggled and said, 'If you would like us to get into an accident I can do that'."
- Jen V

"I had been wanting to go to trance dance but hesitant and trepidatious about it and walked down with you to the labyrinth and had (stupidly) thought that you would maybe need me to walk back up to the cabin with you, since, OMG, it was dark! How would you manage? Duh! But after walking the labyrinth I came out all peaceful and saw you, who had walked it quicker than me, chilling on the grass under the stars with some friends, and when I asked if you wanted to walk back up to the cabin, that I wasn't sure if I should go to trance dance, you so clearly did not need my help … being in your element… and encouraged me to go, and I think the image of you peacefully chatting under the stars stayed with me for trance dance and it ended up being the most meaningful experience of that weekend ritual for me."
- Heather L

These stories illustrate the love that exists in my life. I am grateful for the laughter and acceptance that has always been, and continues to be, a part of my life.

Finding personal acceptance has been a ongoing process through the years. I have not always been comfortable with myself, nor have I always known how to deal with the outside world. I have had some serious medical and social challenges that I have had to fight through in order to succeed. I honestly would not change the cards that were dealt to me.

Today I am a strong, determined woman. Because of my life experiences I have been able to help others, and for that I am grateful. A number of years ago I came to believe that the purpose for my having a disability has been three-fold: I am a student, a teacher, and a lesson.

As a student I have been able to watch and listen to the many things happening around me. I often tell people that my life is a puzzle, and as a student I am learning how everything fits together. As a student I am there to experience life and marvel at it. I have been given tools so that in the future I can go forward and make a difference in the world. Being a student can be difficult at times, because understanding comes slowly.

As a teacher I have been able to educate, mentor and inspire. True teachers have already gone through hard times and now have the opportunity to lead others to a better or easier way. Throughout this process it is important to remember that sometimes one must endure difficulties truly to learn. I once had a conversation with a friend about what can we do for others so they do not have to go through the pain we ourselves have experienced. We had no answer but to stand beside them throughout their journey, so they do not need to travel alone.

Finally, as a living lesson, my life has been instructive to many who take things for granted. My life has helped others to understand how to deal with their own hard times. Through the years I have noticed how many people cannot see the positive light in life unless it is viewed through another person's story. I have come to realize that my role is ever changing, from minute to minute and day to day. Depending on the situation and the people with whom I am interacting I can be any one of the above, or all three at once. For that I am thankful.

Made in the USA
Middletown, DE
13 May 2015